# The Crossroads of a Wonderful Life
## George Q. Langstaff, Jr.
## 1925 - ?

WESTBOW
PRESS®
A DIVISION OF THOMAS NELSON
& ZONDERVAN

WestBow Press books may be ordered through booksellers or by contacting:

WestBow Press
A Division of Thomas Nelson & Zondervan
1663 Liberty Drive
Bloomington, IN 47403
www.westbowpress.com
1 (866) 928-1240

ISBN: 978-1-4908-1377-6 (sc)
ISBN: 978-1-4908-1378-3 (e)

Library of Congress Control Number: 2013919029

Typesetting by Carey Haag

Print information available on the last page.

WestBow Press rev. date: 2/13/2014

## Welcome To My Life

As I look back into the mists of time it fascinates me to observe the many events of my life that were unpredictable, but powerful, in the course of my now eighty seven years. I call them "The Crossroads of My Life." In the book I have attempted to describe for family and friends the most significant events of what I consider a wonderful life. Many of you have played roles in this narrative either directly or indirectly. You may remember events differently but I have tried my best! ☺

It's my hope that those who read the book and look at the over 100 pictures which try to illustrate the many aspects of "Old George's" life will enjoy it. It may even stimulate old memories and encourage you to write a book!? ☺

—George Quigley Langstaff, Jr.

## Philosophy of Life

Yes, I am a Christian and hold my faith close to my heart. Thanks to my Mom and Dad, my Grandmother Irion (Mama) and Grace Episcopal Church in my hometown - Paducah KY. (The Rev Custis Fletcher) I acquired Christian beliefs and practices which I hold dear today. Oh, yeah, I have made some mistakes- Haven't we all?!

In preparing for the publication of my great grandfather Quigley's Journals about which you will read in this book, I found several quotes from his philosophies which I have also tried to follow without ever knowing until the 1990's what he thought and tried to follow. He wrote:

1. Slight not the warm and generous impulse that prompts to good acts for too often quenched it never returns again. December 29, 1859

2. Truth lies at the basis of all true excellence and without it there cannot be greatness. March 20, 1870

3. No time so valueless but it bringeth either good or evil as we ourselves make use of it. August 16, 1872

As you read "The Crossroads" you can grade me on how my results on "The Quigley Philosophies" have been. ☺

# Acknowledgement

During the course of the last eighteen months as I began to consider this book, I have been assisted by several friends and relatives on the memory challenges which arose. My brother, Witt Langstaff, and cousins, Sue Bowman and Witt Irion helped stimulate my memory bank on family and Paducah matters. General Shoe (Genesco) friends Larry Shelton and Bob Richter let me read some of the Genesco Stories to them and they helped fine tune the narrative and correct my name recollections. My in- house editing team of Wife Mickey, Daughters Trish Poole, Lynne Frederick, Kathy Stockman and Grandson Scott Fredrick  have read "The Crossroads"  from cover to cover, corrected spelling, punctuations, syntax,  and accuracy. So, if you find errors you have more than Old George to blame! ☺

Seriously, I deeply appreciate what they have done to help make this book possible. They are not the only family members to help. By the time I was ready to get the typing done, our Grandson, Greg Haag, JR. brought a lovely lady, Carey Foster, to Murfreesboro, TN to be his bride. Our latest "Granddaughter" has done a great job of converting my scribble to readable print. She now says that she knows more about the family than any other "In- Law"!

I have also been pleased with the team from Douglas Printing Co. headed by Nichole Steinhurst and featuring Jim Jarles and Josh Blevins which has done a fine job and been great to work with.

So... All of us thank you for reading "Our Book"! We hope you enjoy it!

# The Crossroads of a Wonderful Life
# Table of Contents

# Chapter 1

## In The Beginning

- Introduction
- Prelude
- Early Crossroads
- The Cabin
- Grace Episcopal Church
- Great Flood of 1937
- How the Flood Saved a Clan
- How the Flood Changed My Life
- Of Girls and Sports
- Mr. Walter Jetton - The Awakening of Leadership Responsibility
- Debate- An Intellectual Team Sport

## Introduction

Have you ever considered the many crossroads of your life? Those times when you made choices to go one way instead of another way? Or to do this rather than that? Have you ever considered what impact these decisions have had on the course of your life and the lives of those you treasure most?

Neither had I until I recently began to examine my own life from the perspective of some 87 years. It's hard to believe how many significant crossroads I have experienced and how they have influenced the course of a wonderful and blessed life.

After much consideration and some hesitation I have decided to try to reconstruct the most important crossroads of "Old George's Life". I hope that the final product will be of interest to family, friends and maybe a few others.

Of course, the first step is to identify the really significant crossroads and then to generate a compelling narrative about the elements of the crossroad and how the road taken impacted the future.

Some of these have to do with the impact on personality, relationships, philosophy of life, personal behavior, etc. and some with complex decisions on new life directions, jobs, activities, etc.

But before we begin this journey, it is important to know something about the environment into which "Old George" was introduced on July 28, 1925!

## PRELUDE

My brothers, (Witt Irion and Quintus Aden), and I were blessed with a wonderful family background and very special parents. Our mother (Katherine Elizabeth Irion) was the first daughter of Methodist Minister John Witt Irion and Kate McGlathery Irion. She was a freshman at Vanderbilt University when her father died, in 1922 at 55, leaving her mother with 5 younger children and very limited financial resources. Mom left Vandy and came to Paducah, KY, where the Methodist Church provided a home for the family. She went to work as a secretary to the owner of Watkins Dry Goods Store to help provide income for the family. Our father (George Quigley Langstaff) lived in Paducah and was one of 5 children of George Langstaff and Ina Quigley. After graduating from Kentucky Military Institute he had returned to Paducah to become involved in the management of Langstaff- Orm Lumber Co., a very successful sawmill/lumber business at the confluence of the Ohio and Tennessee Rivers. All of this was taking place in the early 1920's. It was laying the groundwork for the first great crossroad of my life!

For in early 1924 a coworker at Watkins arranged a blind date for Katherine (then 20) with George Q. Langstaff (then 23). When he arrived to pick her up at 2701 Jefferson St. (not yet paved) he got stuck in the mud and they had to take the trolley to town for their date. The next day he brought a team of mules from "The Mill" to pull the car out of the mud. In spite of this miserable start they fell in love. That summer during a canoe paddle to Livingston Point in the same canoe which still serves the family at Langstaff Landing in Destin, FL George proposed to Katherine and she said "Yes!" My first crossroad had been encountered and a happy direction determined. They were married on October 1, 1924.

Their honeymoon was a classic which started with a train ride from Paducah to Chicago, highlighted by my Grandfather Langstaff's printed flyer handed out to all the passengers. (see Addendum) .Then they traveled through Detroit, Niagara Falls, West Point, New York, Mt. Holly, N.J. (The old Langstaff family home-place after immigration from England) Philadelphia and home to Paducah.

Many years later when Mickey and I lived in Philadelphia we became well acquainted with Mt. Holly and our cousins there. Mom visited us there and, of course, we took her to Mt. Holly to visit the old Langstaff Homeplace (now the Village Library). As we wandered through the house I asked Mom where she and Dad had stayed on their honeymoon visit. She immediately pointed out the upstairs bedroom on the left of the stairs going up. I then posed this question---

"Mom, I've been thinking about your honeymoon and it seems that from the time you left Paducah until you arrived here it was about a month and she said "Yes, that's right!"

And I said "Well, if that's right and since I was born on July 28th I could have been conceived in this very room" and a look of wonder came over her face and she said "Well... It could have been!"
First crossroad defined and verified! George is conceived!! This crossroad could not have been better!! ☺

## EARLY CROSSROADS

Very early memories are hard to resurrect but they also tend to be very significant. As background for my first crossroad I must say a little about our mother. Most who knew her would say that she never met a stranger. She was genuinely interested in people. She had an incredible work ethic. She truly wanted to be a friend. With her sons she was loving; she set sound, meaningful and appropriate goals; she was a great teacher who understood what the lessons needed to be and how to get them absorbed. The family "Rules of the Road" were clear, fair and not to be broken without stern but understood consequences. Her sons could not have had a better mom!

One of her objectives was to help us get sound "Pre-Kindergarten" schooling in many fields but especially in an understanding of our great country, its history, its leaders, etc. So, by my Kindergarten years I had some strong coaching on these matters. Early on, at Andrew Jackson Kindergarten the teacher was reviewing our early days as a nation and asked the class if anyone knew who George Washington was. Well, guess who was ready with the stories of George Washington- the cherry tree- "I cannot tell a lie story" etc. Yep, Old George.

Now why do I mention this as my first real crossroad? It's not because Mom had tutored me well. It's because of the way it made me feel good to be able to excel with my peers. I liked it and, to be honest, I know that it inspired me to want to excel in the years ahead.

And then there was Dad! The business man, the outdoorsman, the athlete, the jokester, the ultimate disciplinarian, the ukulele player, and the one you could talk to about "man" things. He taught us to hunt, fish, swim, canoe, work around the house, drive, play sports, camp, etc. He was a man's man, our best friend!

Dad ushered me through many crossroads but one I never shall forget had to do with being bullied and how one handles that. Our neighborhood was full of kids and Hunter Martin from across the street was a year older. He bossed me around and bullied me constantly. One day he hit me and I ran home crying to Dad who was working in the yard. He looked at me and said something like " What's wrong with you?" and I said " Hunter hit me!" and he said " Son, there are bullies everywhere and if they see that you will cry and run away they will just keep it up. Next time Hunter hits you just whack him back harder than he hit you and see what happens." A couple of days later Hunter whacks me again and instead of crying and running, I whacked him as hard as I could right on the nose. Blood starts spurting. Hunter starts crying and runs home.

Final Results - He never hit me again. I never hit him again. We became lifelong best friends. My response to bullies of any type was permanently changed.

Dad taught us many things (I could do a whole book on them) but how about two more?
HUNTING - He was an avid hunter and the favorite game was dove and quail. I started going with him, carrying my pop gun, when I was about 10. Finally when I was 12 I got a single shot 410 shotgun and learned how to really be a hunter. At about fourteen I was awarded my great uncle's double barrel 12 gauge and now was a true hunting partner - except Dad controlled the ammunition. If the limit was 10 birds I got 11 shells. Of course, the object was to make me a careful and accurate shot and it sure had that effect. If a covey of quail flushed you were very careful to pick your target and aim carefully rather than going bang, bang at the whole covey. I got my limit a number of times but not always. (Dad was better but no hunter is perfect.)

During my competitive TENNIS days I was playing in the Paducah Junior (18 and under) Tournament and reached the finals. My opponent was a fine player whose total athletic focus was tennis. He had been well trained at the country club. My tennis was a "pick up - learn as you go" game. The match was 2 out of 3 sets. We each won a set and in the final set he began to force me on the defensive. I was losing my concentration (The score was 4-1 his favor). As we made the change of courts, Dad motioned me to come over to the fence. He said "Son, you've lost your concentration. You need to focus on what you do best- deep shots and your net game. Now put that in your mind and don't get distracted. Start singing a song to yourself and concentrate on your game" Well, guess what - I started singing my song, hitting deep to his backhand and coming to the net more aggressively. I won the last set 13-11 and took The Cup. Ever since then when I start losing, I sing my song. My buddies kid me about it but it works. Thanks, Dad. During the early years of high school Dad would talk about The Richest Man in Babylon and how he got rich. It was Dad's way of trying to teach us the secrets of effective money management. I half listened and absorbed some of the basics but had no idea where all of this really came from. Years later as I drove to the farm one day, I was listening to Dave Ramsey on the radio and he started talking about a book The Richest Man in Babylon by George S. Clason. That really got my attention! Since my tasks at the farm weren't pressing that day I turned around and headed for the nearest book store. And there it was!

Clason had started writing this collection of parables in 1926 for publication in pamphlets which had a wide distribution to banks, businesses, insurance companies etc. This introduction of Clason's idea by my Dad when I was a teenager has had a major impact on my approach to handling money. And I have preached the concepts to my family and friends far more than they probably wanted to hear! I highly recommend it to you if you haven't read it! P.S. I do not get a commission! ☺

In summary, we were blessed with world class parents who guided our development with intelligence, firmness, patience, Christian faith and tons of love. We were blessed!

## Myrtle Sherrill

And then there was Myrtle Sherrill, our maid, overseer, Boss and confidant. She was Queen of the house when Mom and Dad were not at home. She knew how we were expected to behave and she held us to it. We liked to tease her and one day as I ran through the kitchen I flipped her on the bottom. Was that a big mistake!! ☹ The next thing I knew I was flat on the floor with big Myrtle sitting on top of me and whacking my bottom!

I won't call that a crossroad but it surely taught me an important lesson – Don't flip Myrtle!!
We loved her like a member of the family and stayed in touch with her for many years until her death.

## THE CABIN

In the early 1930's Dad and friend Russell Martin built a one room log cabin on rented land 9 miles above Paducah on the Tennessee River. This was one of the most significant events of my young life. Each summer until I left for the Navy in 1943 we lived at "The Cabin" - swimming, fishing, canoeing, sailing, hunting, entertaining our friends, etc. We learned to live in the woods. We were in extraordinary physical condition and ready to go in the Fall when football season started. As we began to have paying summer jobs we still focused on "The Cabin" for weekends.

I believe "The Cabin" was one of the most important crossroads of my life. It prepared me in so many important ways for the life ahead. It taught skills I have used my whole life. It helped me develop confidence in my ability to function effectively in a broader array of environments than most young men of my era. It enhanced my determination to stay physically and mentally fit which, I believe, has contributed to my longevity. And it created a family bond that lives in my heart every day.

## Grace Episcopal Church

I am a Christian. Not "Born Again" but from my earliest memories. My mother with her strong Methodist family background and my father with his family's historic role in the establishment of Grace Episcopal Church in Paducah set the stage for my lifelong dedication to Jesus Christ and his message to our world. Grace Church was the crucible in which my Christian understanding was nurtured, encouraged and allowed to blossom. Ok - not without many challenges, setbacks, doubts, etc. But under the calm and effective shepherding of the Rev. Custis Fletcher and many wonderful church leaders, my faith became an important element and building block of my life. I consider it a growing and evolving crossroad which is always with me.

## Great Flood of 1937

The early 1930's were a tough time in America. A massive depression starting in 1929 had changed the Langstaffs from a financially well off family to one that was really tightening the strings. Mom had gone to work; the mill had made massive expense reductions, but as things began to get a little better there was growing optimism. Government programs such as C.C.C. and W.P.A. were providing new jobs and doing some good work. By 1935 the mill had begun to again receive timber floated down the Tennessee River, saw it into lumber and stack it along the river to cure. Things were looking up.

I was not much aware of all this since I was only 10 in 1935 and my focus was on school, sports, and having fun (no girls yet). And, so things rocked along.

In early 1937 (now almost 12 years old) there were ominous warnings of potential major floods effecting both the Ohio and Tennessee Rivers simultaneously (Paducah had no flood wall in those days) but there was no panic - there had been floods before. (Previous flood record high was 3 ft. above the bank)

And then early one morning our phone rang at 244 North 38th Street, and it was Dad for me calling from 2nd and Adams (The Mill). He said "Son, get on some work clothes and catch the next bus ( on 35th St.) and get down to The Mill as soon as you can. Do it now!" Well, I knew something big was up and within 10 minutes I was on the way. When I arrived at The Mill I was shocked to see that the river was right up to the edge of the lumber yard. Dad and about 10 of the workmen were cutting chains and metal stakes to length. He explained that my job was to climb on top of the lumber stacks (about 10-12 ft. high), catch the end of the thrown chains, take them across and lower them so that both ends could be secured to the ground with the metal stakes. Of course, the purpose was to keep the lumber (3 years of sawed timber being cured) from floating away. We worked all day. I have no idea how I got back home but I'll never forget that day.

And the water continued to rise and rise and rise. To make the story short - It ultimately exceeded the previous high by some 10 feet! All of our work was for naught! Every stick of lumber was washed away! The flood extended 29 blocks into city. Witt, Quint and I were evacuated to Memphis. Our house became a guest home for relatives with flooded houses.

The Mill never recovered. The loss of its inventory of sawed lumber could not be overcome. I can remember like it was yesterday the night in the summer of 1938, while we were staying at the cabin, that Dad came home for supper and, as we sat around the table, said "Well, today we are starting a new direction in our lives." I asked "What do you mean, Dad?" The answer was "Today we had to shut the mill and take voluntary bankruptcy." He explained that The Mill was permanently closed. He and his brothers and father no longer had jobs. He had $25 from splitting the cash and that was it.

Now that was a crossroad! It was tragic! It was frightening! It was devastating! And it was probably the most important crossroad of my life and that of the entire Langstaff Clan. Why? Well, read the next section on "How the Flood Saved a Clan." And then read "How the flood changed my life."

## How the Flood Saved a Clan

First, a little about the Langstaff "Clan". My great grandfather George Langstaff from Mt. Holly N.J., fresh out of The College of New Jersey (now Princeton University) where he had been Valedictorian of the Class of 1848 and his younger brother, Sam, decided to "go west". They traveled down the Ohio River and on a stop in Paducah, KY they decided to stay and start a business. After several tries and with the help and partnership of an experienced lumberman, John Orm, they founded Langstaff-Orm Lumber Company, It

15

flourished, and it became the employment site of Langstaff men over 3 generations. By the mid 1930's my grandfather, George and his three sons, James, George Q. and Sam were heavily dependent on "The Mill" for their livelihood. Between them the three sons had nine sons coming along with eyes on "The Mill" as their heritage.

And along comes the flood and away goes "The Mill". The end result was that the young clan was thrown out into the world to fend for itself. And they did well:  2 West Point career army officers, 2 doctors, 2 successful business executives, 1 mining engineer, 1 lawyer and a Washington politician/musician/insurance executive.

Had "The Mill" survived I can only imagine the struggle within the family for control. Instead, the family became a cheering squad for each of these nine guys as they went from success to success. And the two lovely girls of the generation, Ina Claire and Susan, each brought terrific husbands to join us and enjoy the cheers. Ironically, "The Clan" was saved by the Flood of 1937!!


### How the Flood Changed My Life

Within a few days after The Mill closed we had a family meeting - Dad, Mom, Me (13), Witt (11), Quint (almost 10).  Dad explained exactly what our financial situation was and what he and Mom were doing to find ways to earn money, to cut back on expenses, etc. And then we explored ways that the boys could contribute. And from that day forward we all worked: I got up at 4:00 a.m. during winter months and serviced the neighbor's furnaces (removed clinkers, filled stokers etc.). I became a babysitter for younger neighborhood kids; in the summer I cut grass and did other yard work. Witt became a paper boy and delivered papers on his bike plus many other odd jobs. Mom and Quint made and sold "Katherine's Cookies" to stores all over town (They were delicious!) on racks Dad had made to hold the cookie sacks. During summers we found work at drug stores, in telegraph delivery, a local dairy - (popsicle dippers, buttermilk makers etc.) and on and on.  Half of whatever we made went into the family pool. And we got by - and it was good for us.

Dad gradually found more and more meaningful work and ultimately got back into the lumber business which he loved and was very good at. But that's for a later crossroad.

The essence of the flood and its impact on my life is simple but very powerful. At 13 I started to work and earn. I learned the importance and value of money. I saw my parents face the impact of going from "well to do" to poverty and how they recovered with hard work, determination and a never failing positive approach to life.

Yep! Those were hard times but they made better men of my brothers and me. A tough crossroad but I'm a better man as a result.

## Of Girls and Sports

The teenage years saw many changes. Crossroads? Well, yes, but more complex and even confusing. Take Girls - The nuisances who were constantly in the way. They couldn't do boy things well but they wanted to be involved. Some were smart and showed you up in class. And, I'll have to admit, some were pretty and I liked to look at them. Why? I wasn't sure. ;)

Now Sports - That's a different thing! I loved sports - football, swimming, baseball, tennis etc. Football and swimming were my favorites. During Junior High Years I played on the Brazelton Junior High football team and learned how to lose! 24 games in 3 years - 1 tie and 23 losses! On swimming I did better with several blue ribbons.

In High School - football was it for me. We had a fine team and excellent coaches. We played top flight teams from Kentucky, Tennessee, Arkansas, Mississippi, and Missouri and won a good percentage. I considered my football years a major crossroad in my life. Not because of a won/loss record or personal awards but because of what I learned about the importance of "The Team" and its ability to work together. I truly believe that my many years of team play in high school and college prepared me for later years in the business world. In those years I participated in many complex situations in an executive capacity which required intricate teamwork from participants from many backgrounds. For better or worse, sports also created in me a strong desire and determination to win.

You all know that I played football but I had decided not to go into more detail about it nor the book which a Paducahan, Bob Swisher, had written A Century of Excellence - describing Paducah Tilghman High School Football performance from 1904-2003. Bob invited football players from many classes to provide fun or serious recollections about their days playing for the "Tilghman Tornado".

Bottom line: I can't resist including my stories in The Crossroads.

## My First Starting Assignment

In 1941, I was a 160 lb. right guard. I had played a good bit but had not started a game and a big game was coming up - Manual at Louisville! Before leaving on a big trip, Coach McRight made some adjustments in the line including moving All Southern Gene Banta from right guard to tackle and taking a chance on starting Langstaff and Willoughby at the guard positions. The big day arrived and here we were starting our first game against one of Kentucky's toughest teams, on their field in front of more people than we had ever seen at a game.

We played the single wing in those days and the guards pulled out one way or the other to lead many plays. On our first possession, Paul Willoughby and I pulled out aggressively to wipe out the opposition but one of us went the wrong way and we ran head on into each other! Talk about embarrassed!

For at least 50 years Paul and I debated who went the wrong way. In spite of our big mistake, we did win the game! (19-14)

**My Greatest Play (for which I was duly toasted by teammates at later reunions)**

It took place at Greenwood, Mississippi (yep, that's right) on a rainy night in 1942. The field had no grass and by the end of the third quarter it was a sloppy mess and we were 7 points down! Finally we drove down the field and scored to make the score 20-19 (as I remember it) with only a few ticks left on the clock. We lined up for the extra point. I was at right guard with a tough, angry Greenwood guy in front of me. As the ball was snapped, he charged right at me. My feet slipped completely out from under me and this big brute charged right over me with his hands thrown up to block the kick. Hal Brown our quarterback and kicker, half slipped and his kick was low. The brute leaped up to block it and hit the ball with a "splat"! To our joy and with his help, the ball was boosted up cleanly between the goal posts and the game ended in a 20-20 tie! I was a hero!

**Mayfield 1942, Thanksgiving Day**

No game was ever as important to us as the Mayfield game. It was the measure of the season. And we had a great season going with only a narrow loss to Memphis Central. So both teams were totally hyped for the big contest. The Mayfield stadium was packed.

On the first play from scrimmage (their ball), I took a knee to the nose (no face masks in those days) which smashed my nose. Blood was pouring out. I knew the knee belonged to Virgil Gilliam. Louis McDonald, our center and later a well-respected coach at Mayfield, looked at me and thought I should go out. But this was Mayfield where a little blood was a badge of honor! A few plays later, I happened to catch Virgil on the chin with my elbow and he suffered a severe cut to his tongue. Now the blood was flowing on both sides of the line. And so it continued for the rest of the game which we won 19-0.

The following week, Virgil and I were selected to play for the West in the Shrine East-West game. When we arrived in Lexington, I had a metal splint in my nose and he had stitches in his tongue. I couldn't breathe and he couldn't talk. The game was played in 25 degree weather with 3 inches of snow and still snowing! And we lost the game! Ain't football fun!?

***

Many years later I was invited to speak to the Mayfield Rotary Club. For my introductory remarks and knowing that Virgil Gilliam, now Mayfield's Mayor, would be in the audience I couldn't resist telling my story about Thanksgiving Day 1942. And I embellished it a good bit! ☺ Virgil jumped up and demanded to tell his side of the story with even more embellishments. The room was rocking with laughter!

Following our 1942 season Virgil was named All-State and I was named All-Southern! (We became good friends and he later helped me set up the Quigley College Scholarships at Mayfield High)

Now about the girls!  By the time I got to high school my attitude toward girls seemed to undergo a considerable change. They didn't seem to be as big a nuisance. Their shapes seemed to have changed for the better. They smelled wonderful. I even got to thinking that a date with one might be fun. I actually took dancing lessons at Miss Crystal's (I wasn't too good but got by).

And the question of a date kept coming up. We had parties where we played games (like spin the bottle) and danced but no real dates. And then about junior year double or triple dating started and that was fun. The girls were nice and actually fun to be with! Sometimes, if the car was crowded, one of them had to actually sit on your lap!

At first it was all double or triple dating and I "dated" several different girls and the dates usually meant a movie and then a soda at Albritton's Drug Store (where I worked for a while). "Smooching" was fun with a few kisses but no serious petting - at least in our gang. We would have been shocked and even horrified at what goes on today!!

Bottom Line - By the end of high school I had a whole new attitude toward girls. There were some out there that I really enjoyed being with - smart, pretty, fun to be around, etc. I might even consider "Going Steady" someday! In due course I'll let you in on two "girl" Crossroads.


### Mr. Walter Jetton (Pussyfoot) and the Awakening of Leadership Responsibility

Walter Jetton, Principal of Tilghman High School, was a major influence on the lives of Tilghman students. He ran a tight ship with his students, teachers and coaches, yet he was not loud and angry in his manner, but steady and quiet in his approach. I attest to the fact that as I entered high school, in one brief encounter, he had a huge and positive impact on me.

John (Bud) Kern, (later an Annapolis Grad and Admiral) and I were close friends from early days and we entered Tilghman with great enthusiasm. Shortly after our arrival we all were assigned hall lockers and our two lockers were side by side. A few days later between classes Bud and I were scuffling around in the hall and knocked a fire extinguisher off its cradle. It started spraying.  Bud grabbed it and started spraying me. I took it away and started spraying him and anyone else in reach. The class bell rang and we hurried to class leaving the exhausted extinguisher to fend for itself.

19

It seemed that we had barely gotten seated when the door opened and a messenger from the principal's office handed a note to the teacher. She opened it, looked at me, looked at Bud and read - "George Langstaff, Bud Kern go to the principal's office - NOW!"

Needless to say we were scared to death but hurried downstairs to the principal's office. His secretary ushered us into his empty office and told us to sit in the two chairs facing his desk. And there we sat for what seemed an eternity. The door finally opened and Mr. Jetton, in his tippy-toe fashion, glided over to his desk. He looked long at each of us. Addressing Bud he said, "Bud Kern, Valedictorian of his Senior Class at Brazelton" And then at me "George Langstaff, President of his Senior Class at Brazelton. "Long pause" - I expected more of you two!" And then he glided out of the office.

Without question it was the most powerful rebuke I ever received. Both of us took it to heart. Bud was Valedictorian of our senior class two years later; I was President of the Junior Class and President of the Student Body in our senior year. Until he died many years later, Mr. Jetton stayed in touch with both of us and the careers we pursued. I can truly say that he created an important crossroad in my life.

### Debate- An Intellectual Team Sport and Its Influence on Me

As sports go, my key high school interests were football (in the fall) and swimming (in the summer). Basketball was the spring sport but, in-spite of lots of effort, I really wasn't worth a darn. One day Mr. Snodgrass, a teacher who was the forensics coach, asked me if I would consider trying debate. It seemed that Creed Black (one of my lifelong best friends and my competition in class elections) was the star debater. However, debate teams require two debaters. So, the idea was that when we were debating on the positive side Tommy Smith would be Creed's partner; and on the negative side, I would be the partner. It was a Spring "sport" and I had already done a fair amount of speaking. So we set out on what became one of my most rewarding high school activities.

Creed was incredibly good. He assimilated, organized and expressed his arguments in almost a professional manner. Tommy and I became better and better as we learned from him. I loved it. Here was a new "sport" that was highly competitive, required extensive research, organization, practice etc. and produced winners -- and losers! In our senior year we won the Region in our state and were runners-up in the State Competition. Creed went on to become a noted newspaper reporter, editor, and publisher. From my viewpoint this was one of my most productive high school activities since it prepared me for a career which required public speaking skills as well as the analytical review and analysis of complex issues. A crossroad taken!

# Chapter 2

## **The Navy and a Girl**

- December 7, 1941/ WWII
- Grandfather Langstaff Dies
- Paducah, KY
- NROTC - University of South Carolina
- Ground Hog Day
- The Girl at the Piano

### December 7, 1941 and WWII

Without any question the Japanese attack on the United States was a crossroad and a game changer for every American. From my point of view it brought me to the conclusion that as soon as high school was over I intended to attend the U.S. Naval Academy and have a career in the Navy. During senior year 1942-43 I worked hard to make application and get the support of a Kentucky Senator or Representative ,but, in the final analysis I did not get an appointment. So I enlisted in The Navy V-12 program and on June 3, 1943, I went to Fort Knox, KY to pass the physical test, be sworn in, and get my assignment orders. Much to my surprise and disappointment the assignment officer said, "Son, our classes are full and we can't take you until the November class." In shock I said "But, Sir, I'm ready to go now. My bag is packed for me to go today." And he said "Well, you just go on back home and your orders will be sent there." And reporting for duty was postponed until November. I was very disappointed and headed back home to Paducah. The delay itself was a crossroad that had an enormous impact on my life both short and long term. So there I was at home. The whole summer lies ahead. Most of my buddies have left for service in one branch or another. What am I going to do now?

Within a couple of days I got a call from the manager of the Paducah Country Club asking if I would like to be the club pool life guard for the summer- and it paid. How could I turn it down?! It was a summer to remember! I somehow felt a little guilty but I surely enjoyed it. Here I was almost the only guy my age left in town. The pool was alive with good looking young girls and I'm the one sitting up there in the lifeguard chair.

I was dating a little but nothing serious. My focus was on getting myself in the best possible condition, playing as much tennis as possible, canoeing, hunting etc. And then one day in early July a beautiful girl I had never seen before comes walking by my chair and stops to speak with several girls that I did know. Before the day was over I knew a lot about her - Lou Rutter, from Cincinnati, visiting an aunt who lived a few blocks away, wasn't dating anyone- etc. etc. It didn't take long before I met her and asked for a date.

Before her visit was over we were dating regularly. She met and visited with my family. We went with groups to the cabin, canoed on the river. Before her summer in Paducah was over we were beginning to feel a commitment.

In September, I finally got my orders to report on November 1, 1943 to a V-12 Unit at Emory University in Atlanta. Lou returned to Paducah from Cincinnati to see me off. I considered her my girl and so did my family. After I got to Emory we continued to talk by phone often and to write almost daily. During the Christmas leave I took the train to Cincinnati and spent a couple of days with Lou and family before going home for a few days. All went well.

During the months of January and February (1944) I struggled with how to direct my Navy Career, since it again appeared, I would not get an Annapolis appointment. For months I had considered what seemed to me to be "A Call" to direct my life toward the Christian Ministry. Within the Navy Unit at Emory there was a small group going thru the same process and I joined them.

During that struggle I kept Lou fully informed and let her know when I actually made application for the Navy Chaplaincy Corps, She obviously shared that information with her mother. And then I received the letter - in service it was called a "Dear John Letter." The gist of the letter was that her mother would not permit her to continue to write me or talk on the phone much less visit with me. We were through! "Do not write! Do not call! No preachers in our family!" What a shocker that was! You might call it a mighty crash on that crossroad of a life!

I gradually recovered from the shock and went on about my Navy training at Emory. Toward the end of the spring semester I received notice that I was not being accepted to the Chaplaincy Corps. But was being accepted to the Naval R.O.T.C Program at the University of South Carolina reporting June 1, 1944. This was the next best to Annapolis as prep for a Navy career. So I went with enthusiasm but without a girlfriend.

## Grandfather Langstaff Dies

I had barely gotten to my NROTC duty in Columbia, S.C. when I received a call from home, Grandfather Langstaff had died. The funeral was to be in 3 days. I knew that I would make it if only I could get a 5 or 6 day pass. And that pass had to be issued by Chief Milady, a tough, wizened Chief Petty Officer whom I had only viewed from a distance.

When I made my plea about the grandfather for whom I was named he looked straight at me then up at the ceiling as though saying to himself "What Next?" But I like to think it was a voice up there saying "Do it" because this led to an important crossroad for our family. And he signed the pass!

Now, how to get there in time. I had enough money to take the bus as far as Knoxville, TN (Overnight) and early the next day start hitchhiking. By afternoon of that day I was in Nashville and finally found my way to the highway to Kentucky. A car with a husband and wife picked me up and said they were going to Hopkinsville. Good ride. Their name was "Bass". When he heard mine he asked if my father was the one who had been in the lumber business in Paducah. "Yes, sir".  " What is he doing now?", He asked. I explained Dad's succession of jobs since the bankruptcy and that he was now a supervisor at the new Ordnance Factory. "Well, do you think he would be interested in getting back into the lumber business?" Mr. Bass was owner of Bass & Co. a successful business in Hopkinsville and was considering opening a branch in Paducah.

I was overjoyed but simply said that I would ask Dad as soon as I got home and he would call Mr. Bass. Of course, Dad called. They hit it off. Dad opened a successful branch in Paducah and in a short time was asked to open a larger branch in Nashville. The branch was also successful and is where Dad completed his working career many years later. Well, how about that for a crossroad?!

## Paducah, KY

Before getting too far away on my Navy journey and related crossroads I must say a few words about my hometown. Paducah KY, my home for 18 years, still holds a treasure chest of fond memories for me. Ask Mickey and she will tell you that I cannot resist telling her over and over when we are in Paducah what happened here or there. One day we both will be there permanently side by side with my Mom and Dad, brother Quint, great grandfather Quintus Quincy Quigley and his family, aunts and uncles, etc. on the Quigley Family plot in Paducah Oak Grove Cemetery.

Paducah was ideal for a young boy who loved the outdoors - three beautiful and bountiful rivers; unlimited acres of woods and fields available to hunters; a world class public park- swimming, tennis, softball, picnic areas etc. And all only a short bike ride away.

But its most important feature as I look back was the quality and effectiveness of its public schools. The system was headed by H.L. Smith, a very strong and intelligent executive. As the impact of the depression took hold and more and more good people were out of work, he seized the opportunity to build a truly top flight teacher cadre from grades one to high school. They were terrific! Highly qualified – tough but fair - genuinely interested in the students - made learning fun (most of the time). An example of "Not Fun" – as a music requirement, I had a class under Miss Ann Gannaway. I tried but it wasn't pretty. When my grade came it was D-. I went to Miss Ann and asked why it was so low and she replied – "George, that was a gift!" Fortunately that was my only music class. Oops, I forgot one other experience.

Our dad was a saxophone player and when I was in Junior High we thought it would be good if I went out for the band. Dad had been giving me some pointers. Mr. Burt, the high school band director would visit the 3 junior high schools to give lessons and to identify prospects for the Tilghman High School Band. After about 6 visits he asked me to stay after the practice. His message was short and precise. "George, I think it would be best for you to stick with football". It didn't take a genius to get that message!

But seriously, I believe the education I received in the small town of Paducah (30,000) prepared me to compete effectively in college with students from any background. My early "education crossroad" was positive.

## NROTC- University of South Carolina

I arrived in Columbia, SC about June 1, 1944. This was a full-fledged state university which, on the male side, was now almost 100% military. The intriguing thing was that it also had most of the aspects of a regular university - fraternities and sororities, athletics (football, basketball, swimming, and track etc.etc.). The military (Naval) training was intense and demanding with excellent instructors.

As a newcomer who didn't know anyone, it was lonely at first. Soon I was invited to several fraternity rush parties and ultimately pledged Sigma Nu. It was a good choice for me since several members were also football players. I had gone out for football as soon as practice started. Things were looking up. I got to play a lot although I was not a starter. Our season was ok but not perfect. But I was playing again!

One day in the Fall I went to the YMCA room at lunch break where the students gathered, danced, sang, flirted, etc. As I watched the dancing it became apparent that a girl over in one corner at a piano was playing for the dancers. Someone would call out a song and bam! She could play it! No music to read. She just banged it out! And she was really cute!! But, shy as I was I didn't go meet her. ☺

And Navy life went on: Nav- Learning to navigate; Naval History and strategy; geography; math; etc. Then active training; rifle; marching; seamanship; physical training; etc.

I had a few dates but I had become rather wary of girls and didn't make much effort to connect.

## Groundhog Day

Groundhog day of February 1945 was an important Sigma Nu day because it was a custom to have a dinner party celebrating the Groundhog! DUH!

My roommate, Bob Tindall, insisted that I had to bring a date and his girlfriend's suite mate might go with me. I didn't know her but he said she was pretty and was the drum majorette for the band. So what the heck, I said "Fine".

On Groundhog Day I went to Sims Dormitory to pick up my unknown date. After checking in and giving the attendant my name and my date's name I sat and waited. Soon I heard the attendant call my name. As I walked to the desk I did a double take because there with a big smile stood The Girl at the Piano! Wow! Little did I know then what a tremendous crossroad this would be!!

## The Girl at the Piano

Her name was Mickey Black and she was not just pretty she was beautiful! I was impressed. We chatted as we walked a few blocks to the pre-dinner reception. She asked what I planned to do in the Navy and I told her about my efforts to get an appointment to Annapolis and, having failed that so far, my struggle with the chaplaincy question. Much to my surprise she thought the chaplaincy was a good objective. For some reason, that really got my attention☺!

The Groundhog Dinner at a downtown hotel was a great success - good food, fun, good friends, great discussions, etc. And before leaving Mickey at the dorm I asked for another date.

This led to another, another, etc. Four months packed with trips to the river, movies, pizza on the library steps (since Navy guys had to stay on campus, the girls would collect the money, get the pizzas and bring them back to waiting gobs). And the first kiss at the observatory. I say that she asked me, she says "Baloney, girls don't ask boys!" Oh well, it was fun!! One of our activities was badminton and together we won the campus mixed doubles. Still have the trophy.

About mid-April we were really getting serious. I had two more semesters to go on campus. So lots of good times ahead and then guess what! A notice came that I had finally received an appointment to Annapolis! "Report for physical right away (Charleston) and if you pass, report to Annapolis on June 1."

What the heck do I do now? The war in Europe is winding down. Our full Military and Naval forces will soon be unleashed on Japan (no knowledge yet of the atomic bomb). I'm 2 semesters away from becoming a Navy Ensign but not with the Annapolis "Guarantee" of a meaningful Navy career. And I really wanted that! And I'm in love!

I struggled with the decision. Finally, the decision was made for Annapolis – my dream for several years. Mickey was supportive and we promised to stay in close touch. I gave her my Sigma Nu pin to remind her .And so I left in late May for a new venture. Another crossroad faced, pondered, struggled with and finally decided. Will it be the right thing to do? Father time will tell!

# Chapter 3

# <u>Annapolis</u>

- Annapolis
- Plebe Football
- The Big Decision
- Civilian Transition

## Annapolis

Wow! Impressive! Magnificent site! Tough discipline! Obey orders! I am back to the bottom of the heap! But this is what I asked for - so shut up and be a midshipman!

Plebe summer was great- No upper classmen. We organized and ran a pretty good ship. Heavy emphasis on Navy fundamentals: seamanship, sailing, drilling, firearms, signaling, some book work, etc.

Then the upperclassman returned. We were reorganized by companies and brigades and moved to new locations in Bancroft Hall based on the organization. Upper classman were now in charge and they could be a real pain. But that is the system and it serves a purpose.

During August there was a call to plebes for those who wanted to try out for football. During the war both Annapolis and West Point were in position to acquire some of the finest players in the nation. For example, the Navy varsity had 6 guys who had already been All-American at other colleges.

When plebes gathered on the field the coach lined us all up and prepared to eyeball each man and decide who to keep and who to send down to the "Plebe Squad". Keep in mind that I had been a high school All- Southern and had played for South Carolina the previous year. As the coach went down the line he pointed to a man and said "Ok" (he could stay) or "Out" (go play with the Plebes). When he came to me he said "Out". I was shocked and I said "Coach, you haven't even seen what I can do" and he said "Son, you're just too small" I weighed 160 and was a guard. He was right but I didn't like it. So I went to the Plebe Squad.

Meanwhile school cranked up and I got to see and experience this fantastic institution at work. Its purpose is to select the finest candidates, subject them to intense study of all things Navy, create in them the wisdom, experience, good judgment, determination, discipline and people skills to lead men in the management of battle. And they know how to do it! I was impressed and loved it.

Discipline for Plebes was extreme. The slightest violation brought demerits or physical punishment "Drop and give me 50!" meaning drop to the ground and do 50 push-ups or at meals "shove out" which means shove your chair out but remain in the seated position with no chair for the rest of the meal, and many more.

But sometimes it got funny. At assembly your uniform of the day had to be correct and spotless. At one Bancroft Hall outdoor assembly the uniform was dress whites and I had made certain that my uniform was perfect. We were standing at attention as the Admiral made his inspection. Not a muscle moved as he moved down the line toward me. His aide with a notebook was prepared to note violations. As the Admiral inspected the midshipman next to me I felt something whack my hat, run down off of my nose onto my chin and down onto my heretofore spotless uniform. I didn't move a muscle. When the Admiral turned to look me in the eye I could see a flash of anger in his eyes and then when he observed what had really happened, he couldn't hold back his laughter. The pigeons of Bancroft Hall had scored a direct hit. And the Admiral said "Okay, Midshipman, break ranks and go get yourself cleaned up." No Demerits! Unless they gave them to that darn pigeon. ☺

I had several friends from previous days at Annapolis. Bud Kern, my high school buddy and participant in the "Fire Extinguisher Incident" had gotten his appointment the year before I did. Tommy Smith of my high school debate team had also received his appointment in Bud's Class. As "upper classmen" they always threatened me with hazing plans but it was all in fun. Howard House, a fraternity brother from South Carolina, was in my class. He was a top flight basketball player and was already working out with the team. I stayed in touch with them as much as I could. Plebes don't have much freedom.

With the advent of V-J Day we began to realize that there would of necessity be many changes in the Navy. It would put greater and greater emphasis on academic and naval training performance to obtain the top assignment upon graduation. I was bound and determined to become a Line Officer not a Supply Officer. To me at that stage, Line Officers commanded the ships, devised and carried out the battle plans. Supply Officers were off somewhere in a warehouse and didn't really get involved with ships, planes and fighting men. After some 53 years in the business world I now realize that without an effective supply system you are in deep trouble. But at the age 19-20 supply was not for me.

## Plebe Football

It was good to be back on a football field. I was pleased and surprised at the quality of the Plebes. We had some good, hard-nosed practice sessions. Little did I know that one of these sessions would produce perhaps the biggest and most significant crossroad of my life!

The coach had created two teams to square off in a full scale scrimmage and we were all excited about it. In those days uniforms and equipment were way below today's standards. For example, no one had a face mask. Helmets were pitiful compared to modern ones.

The scrimmage was on November 19 as I recall. It was a pretty good battle. Well matched. I played right guard. On the play I will describe, my team was on defense and the ball was about midfield. The play was a fullback plunge over their left tackle. I successfully eluded my blocker and hit the fullback on his right side as hard as I could. Bill Mills, our right defensive end had also eluded his blocker and delivered a strong tackle from the other side. Only one problem! His left hand collided with my head and a finger went deep into my right eye. I was knocked out for a few minutes. As I came to I heard Bill (or someone) say "Oh my God! His eye is knocked out of the socket" Well, that got me awake That wasn't correct. The blow had

29

forced the eye lash deep into the socket behind the eyeball. I was immediately carried into "sick bay". The corpsman on duty got the lash corrected, examined the eye, saw no further problem and sent me back to my dorm room.

My next conscious memory was waking a day later in the hospital with a concussion. I had fainted in a hall on the way back to my room. I stayed in the hospital for a few days and then went back to regular duty but was still in consultation with the doctor on staff due to a dilation problem of that right eye. Two Big Events- the Army-Navy Game and Christmas Leave- were coming up so I pushed the eye problem aside.

What a great experience the game was- the whole Annapolis student body traveled on a ship from Annapolis to Philadelphia. A terrific game. Then meeting cousin Tom Langstaff (West Point) at centerfield after the game and exchanging cuff links. Tom and I grew up together and were like brothers. Tom's older brother James (Pete) was a West Point grad and "Tommy" followed him and became an Air Force fighter pilot (More on Tom later.)

After the game the "Paducah Boys" from both academies and dates met for a fine dinner at an upscale Philadelphia hotel. My date was Mickey's college suite mate who lived just out of Philly. We really had a great time.

But the eye was giving me problems. When my Aunt Faith (Dad's oldest sister and a brilliant lady executive way ahead of her time) heard about the injury she insisted that I must go to a top flight eye specialist at Johns Hopkins, not far from Annapolis. She arranged it for the first day of my Christmas leave.

I was impressed with Johns Hopkins and the doctor. (My brother Quint would graduate from Johns Hopkins years later) After a very complete exam he concluded that the eye still had correctable vision with glasses but that the blow had frozen the dilating function of the right eye damaging my night vision. I had been experiencing that and now I knew why. "Can it be cured?" I asked. His reply was not encouraging. Basically, it was that he considered it unlikely. Traumatic injuries to the eye such as this were hard to reverse.

Having gone through several intense eye exams in my quest for an Annapolis appointment I knew that the injury could have a major impact on my career. And I was worried!

But this was Christmas and I was going home! I had great visits with family and friends. I did a little hunting with Dad and my brothers. Fantastic dinner at Mama's (my Mom's mother) with probably 25 at the table. No dates because my focus was on Mickey and the chance to see her at the last stop on my leave. Uncle Witt Irion (Mom's oldest brother) gave me a great ride to Nashville where he was preparing to join Harvey's, a fine Nashville department store. From Nashville it was hitchhike or bus (at night). I made it in a day and a half. And much to my joy the welcome from Mickey and her family was terrific! After a wonderful visit Mickey and her Dad saw me off at the train station in Columbia.

The trip back to the academy was not a joy. I knew that I had to share the Johns Hopkins report with Academy officers and doctors and I was very concerned about what would happen.

The Academy doctor reviewed the report, and then discussed the report with the Brigade Commander who called me in for a meeting. The bottom line was a full review of my record and my long battle to get to Annapolis and prepare for a full navy career. He honestly shared with me the impact the injury would have on the Line Officer career I wanted. The bottom line, as I had feared, was that my loss of adequate night vision would prevent me from becoming a Line Officer. He explained the importance that supply officers were to the Navy's Mission.

## The Big Decision

When I asked what my options were he said I could continue at the academy through graduation and become a naval officer and accept a supply assignment or since the war was over and pressure for new officers was greatly reduced I could receive an honorable discharge and go back to civilian life.

Oh, My Gosh! Now what? On one side, my long time ambition could not be reached. On the other side, a whole new opportunity was opened: back to civilian life; select a civilian university, seriously court Mickey; etc. You can imagine the vigorous discussion that followed with my family, respected friends, those who helped me get the Annapolis appointment, etc.

I soon came to the conclusion that I should resign, determine the possibility of entering The University Of The South (Sewanee) and prepare for a civilian profession. I had experienced Sewanee through an Episcopal Youth Program when I was in high school and liked it a lot.

When I talked to the Brigade Commander he escorted me to the Commandant for further discussion. Both gave me their Ok and within two weeks I was a new civilian. It was about January 20 to the best of my memory.

Mom had been vigorously at work with Sewanee - even calling the Vice Chancellor, Doctor Guerry. To my joy and surprise I was admitted to Sewanee for the spring semester of 1946. What a fantastic new crossroad in my life!

There was quite a celebration in Paducah when I got home about January 22, 1946. I had a guilty feeling about leaving the Navy but family and friends kept assuring me that I had made the right decision. So on with the new life!

## Civilian Transition

My first challenge was to acquire adequate civilian clothes. I had been in Navy uniforms for over 2 years and before that my civilian supply was pretty bare, plus the fact that I had grown some. Tantoo, a great aunt, set me up to a new suit. Mom and Dad helped out a lot. Sewanee required jacket and tie on campus which complicated matters. Since I had to be on campus by February 6 we did some fast scrambling! And I arrived by train on time!!

# Chapter 4

# <u>Sewanee with a Bride</u>

- Sewanee, The University of the South

- My Brothers

- Life at Sewanee

- The Academic Major

- Finances/Work Possibilities

- Courting Mickey

- Deck Hand on The Motor Vessel Celeste

- A Summer Crossroad

- Sewanee Fall Semester 1946

- The Wedding

- Newlyweds at Sewanee

## Sewanee, The University of the South

For any reader who has not visited Sewanee I can assure you that a visit would impress you enormously. First of all, it rests on top of a beautiful mountain some 50 miles west northwest of Chattanooga, Tennessee surrounded by a magnificent 10,000+ acre forest preserve. Its buildings are reminiscent of European architecture. The students on campus sported jackets and ties with upperclassman (gownsmen) also in academic black gowns. They were all male in those days. Some 550 in total.

The university is owned and managed by thirteen dioceses of the Episcopal Church. St Luke's Theological Seminary is nearby on the mountain as is Saint Mary's Monastery. For me the prevailing Christian focus was impressive. As I came to know the faculty (and based on my exposure to Emory, University of South Carolina, and Annapolis) I was surprised and impressed with its quality and dedication. This was no "backwoods school". These people knew their business!

I was soon in discussion with a counselor as to what academic path I should follow based on what I had already accomplished and what objective I wished to set for myself. My credits thus far placed me as a rising junior but most of my Navy "majors" would not work for a Sewanee major so I had much to do to select a major and then carry a heavy load to make it work. (More on this later.)

The incoming student body was almost all vets so I felt comfortable with them although somewhat sorry that my service record did not measure up to most of them.

One very positive development was that the Sigma Nu Fraternity was on the campus, but with only two Sigma Nu members, one returning vet who had been at Sewanee before military service and me, a transfer from South Carolina! He and I hit it off great and together with 2 very active alums, Charlie Thomas and Arthur Ben Chitty we set out to rebuild the chapter.

And so a new life begins on the mountain! Now where will this crossroad take me?!

But before going any further with my story I want to tell you about two important people in my life - my brothers - Witt and Quint!

## My Brothers

I was only 22 months old when Witt Irion Langstaff was born on May 14, 1927 and I don't remember one thing about the big event. But I was 40 months old when Quintus Aden Langstaff was born on November 27, 1928 and I played a role in that big event. Back in those days most babies were born at home, and the doctor would come there for the big event. Of course, there was great excitement around the house as Mother's delivery got closer and closer. All attention was focused on her and no one paid any attention to me. So I hid in Mom and Dad's closet where I had a good view of Mom's bed through the key hole.

After a while Dr. Pulliam arrived and prepared for the delivery. Shortly, he must have heard me in the closet. He opened the door, saw me, took me by the ear and pulled me out of the closet and into the hall. And I protested in a loud voice "But Doctor Pulliam I want to see the stork!" They never let me forget it!

These were two great brothers! Three boys! Each with his own characteristics, talents, personality, objectives, etc. But brothers who supported one another throughout our lives. OK, so as the oldest, I may have picked on them some or taken advantage when I could. But I loved and respected them even when we had big differences of opinion. We shared two great teachers - Mom and Dad - who kept our differences from becoming major problems.

As we grew up, Witt was always the best organized and the best at the use of his time. During the school year he studied some every night. Quint and I tended to be "crammers" who scrambled just before exams to get by. Guess who produced the best result! and who created a great career at Eastman Chemical Products!

Quint was the one who had the clearest vision of what he intended to do with his life. I can remember him as a little kid with his doctor bag labeled "Dr. Langstaff" administering medicine (sugar pills) to one and all. And after Johns Hopkins and Duke University he became a brilliant and dedicated physician.

All three of us loved sports. You name it, we did it. When I was a high school senior football player Witt was my substitute at right guard and went on to play 4 years of excellent football at Georgia Tech. Quint became a very successful quarterback and after Tilghman played 4 years at Johns Hopkins.

I could go on and on about my brothers. I will simply summarize by saying that I am proud of them and what they have done with their lives – careers - families. Sure, we have had our differences but I am very pleased to be their brother.

### Life at Sewanee

As I settled into life at Sewanee a number of issues presented themselves:

- What major?
- Finances/ Work possibilities
- Courting Mickey
- Steam boating on the Mississippi
- Sigma Nu

### The Academic Major

After a review of Sewanee's academic majors I concluded that "Economics" was as close as I could get to "Business Administration" which was my initial target. Everything I heard about Dr. Eugene Kayden was intriguing - Harvard PhD, tough, dedicated Russian immigrant, favorite with his students. So I signed on and never regretted it.

### Finances/Work Possibilities

The G.I. Bill covered tuition, room and board and fees plus $90 per month paid to me so I was barely ok. But to give me some extra for things like "courting Mickey", clothes, etc., I looked for extra jobs. Ultimately, I became Dr. Guery's file clerk and Director of Intramural Athletics. These paid a few dollars and helped.

### Courting Mickey

From the time I arrived in Sewanee Mickey and I talked by phone almost every day. This was costly but, since her Dad was a Southern Bell Executive we got a break on many calls by calling collect.

The big challenge was that about once a month after Friday classes (11 to 12 a.m.) I set out hitch hiking from Sewanee to Columbia to see Mickey. I would get to Columbia early Saturday, spend Saturday and Saturday night with the Blacks, and start hitchhiking back to Sewanee Sunday morning. Ain't love grand!

On one occasion Mickey and her friend Mary Knowles, came by bus to Sewanee for a weekend dance. Lots of fun! (We can't remember the exact date!) Mickey wowed my fraternity brothers!

In May of '46 Mickey was crowned May Queen of the University of South Carolina. I was one proud guy but jealous of all those guys over there who could see her every day. I got even by asking her to go to Paducah with me to meet my family and she accepted. She actually skipped her graduation ceremony to make the trip.

We had a wonderful bus trip with time to talk and begin to get serious about the future. Mickey was a big hit with my family and friends and vice versa. I had made a strong effort to get family and friends to avoid any references to Lou Rutter and they did well. When we left to come back to Columbia I was very pleased at how warmly Mickey had been received. All looked good!

Cousin Tommy Langstaff was on his way back to West Point and we traveled with him to Oak Ridge, Tennessee on our trip back to Columbia. We stopped there with Cousin Sue Langstaff and family. At breakfast the next morning with a bunch of us around the table Tommy turned to Mickey and pointing to the salt said " Please pass the salt, Lou" The only slip up on the trip. Oh, well I tried! Fortunately, Mickey forgave him (and me!).

For summer break I had secured a job as a <u>deck hand on the motor vessel, "Celeste",</u> which towed oil barges from Helena, Arkansas to Wood River, Illinois on the Mississippi River. The deal was that you worked two months without a break and then received pay for another month without work. Since the boat had no phones I would scramble for a pay phone to call Mickey whenever we docked. I wrote letters to her but it was difficult to get reliable delivery of her letters to me. My loneliness helped stimulate a master plan.

Point one – I really wanted to marry Mickey

Point Two- I was making good money on the boat with no way to spend it

Point Three – My summer work would wind up in Paducah where I knew the owners of Nagel and Myers Jewelry Store.

Point Four- Why not buy an engagement ring and surprise Mickey when I visited with her in Columbia before going back to Sewanee!!

Guess what! I did it! She said yes! We were engaged!!<u>What a summer crossroad!</u>

My family and Mickey's family were very pleased and discussions about wedding timing, location etc. were soon underway. December of 1946 during Christmas break was the target. Mickey and her mom were in charge. I was consulted from time to time but basically, I went back to school. So a little more about Sewanee, Sigma Nu, classes Etc.

## Sewanee Fall Semester 1946

To say that I was a busy guy would be a great understatement. In addition to a very heavy class load I had become Commander (President) of the Sigma Nu chapter. From 2 members in February we had expanded to 34 after a very successful rush season. The two of us were assisted by 2 alums and 2 volunteers from the neighboring Kappa Alpha Fraternity. I had also started to work in the Vice-Chancellor's Office a couple of hours a day.

My main wedding assignment was to reserve an apartment for us in the new married student's complex being created from the abandoned Navy V-12 barracks.

And, of course, I was talking to Mickey at least daily and also made a few weekend hitchhikes to Columbia.

In spite of all this my grades continued to hover around B+ (91.5%) which I thought was pretty good all things considered. ☺

## The Wedding and Honeymoon

And, before long it was early December and time to do some serious last minute wedding planning. I had asked brother Witt to be my Best Man. Brother Quint, Mickey's brothers John and Ken plus a couple of Navy buddies would be ushers. Since I didn't have a tux I replaced the gold buttons on my Navy Blue uniform and it looked OK. Also, I had no car but Dad was letting me use his for the honeymoon- one problem was that it had a small crack in the engine block so about every 75 miles you had to add water to the radiator. Our packing had to include a five gallon can of water and a smaller can for dipping water from the nearest creek. ☺

I met Mom and Dad in Nashville for the trip to Columbia on December 25. Russell and Mary Martin joined our caravan since they would bring Mom and Dad back with them after the wedding. Brother Witt had gone AWOL from Ft. Dix and hitchhiked to Nashville where he also joined the caravan and rode over with Russ and Mary. Quint was also with us and we had a fine trip during which we planned a different way to introduce Quint to Mickey's family. For years Quint had perfected his impersonation of an ape. When he put on his act-including picking lice off of his viewers - you would think he was the real thing. So we decided to put Quint in the car trunk when we got a few blocks from the Black's home and then let me introduce Mom and Dad when we arrived. With that done I would then explain that my brother Quint was with us but he required special care. When I then opened the trunk and Quint jumped out grunting, sniffing everybody and picking lice as he shuffled from one to another, I thought Mickey's Mom would faint! Her face was something to behold! I could only imagine what was going through her mind!! Mickey's Dad caught on right away and was roaring with laughter. Mother Black finally realized what was happening and showed an uneasy smile. She got over it but never let me forget that "nasty trick"! She and Quint became good friends.

My memory of what else went on that final day before the wedding day is very fuzzy. So many last details, friends arriving and checking in, Etc. I do remember a final "date" that night with Mickey. We decided that we still loved each other!!

The wedding service on December 27 at Washington Street Methodist church went great with many friends and family there to support us. We both said "I do" with no reservations.

The reception at the Black's home was well attended and lots of fun. That is until it was time for us to leave. When we came out the front door under a shower of rice Mickey saw the car and stopped dead in her tracks "We can't go in that thing! Look what they have done to the car!" My buddies had done a masterful job of printing messages from front to back capped off with long strings of cans stretching out behind. Finally I said something like "Well, Honey, I'm going in the car and hope you will go with me. I do promise to get it washed as soon as I can find a car wash." Hooray! She decided to go! And away we went!

Many cheers! Our objective was Greenville, S.C. some 100 miles away. I had made reservations at the Poinsett Hotel, the best in Greenville. We arrived about 11:00 p.m. after I got the car washed. That night we became true and complete lovers.

About 6:00 a.m. – Bang! Bang! Bang! On the door. I leaped out of bed and flew to the door. As I started to open it a maintenance man burst in with a tool box in each hand and shouting "There's an emergency in this room!" Mickey is sitting up in the bed with the covers pulled up to her chin!

And then it dawns on me! My darn fraternity brothers have arranged this! When I started laughing so did the maintenance guy. A wedding prank well executed!! I never got a full admission of guilt from my buddies but I know who it was.

The next day we headed up into the mountains to our next stop –Gatlinburg; Tennessee, a famous mountain resort. The accommodations at Gatlinburg Inn were excellent and we had a fine two day stay. Little could we imagine that many years later during her college years our first daughter, Trish, would be the lead singer in a Birmingham - Southern College Group, "The Hilltop Singers", that entertained tourists like us in the evenings at Gatlinburg! Needless to say that drew us back to Gatlinburg a number of times.

Our plan was to travel to Nashville on the, 30th, stop for a night ,and drive to Paducah on the morning of the 31st in time for a New Year's Eve party which Mom was arranging with all of my friends. We stopped at the Alamo Plaza in Nashville which provided easy access to the highway to Paducah. Even with no interstates in those days the drive took at most 3 ½ - 4 hours, so, we awakened at 7:00a.m. and looked out the window - Holy smokes! There was a least 10 inches of snow and still snowing. My mind was racing - now what do we do?!

I knew that North and Northwest of Nashville on the regular highway there were imposing hills which, with no chains, could be a real challenge. But going straight west for about 75-80 miles on the Memphis Highway the land was relatively flat and then there was a good highway going northwest to Paducah with few big hills. And I decided to go the Memphis Highway and avoid the hills. It proved to be what Dad called "the dumbest decision a normally intelligent boy ever made!"

We made the first leg of about 75 miles to Huntington in good shape. The snow had stopped and there didn't seem to be as much on the road so I turned north toward Paris, Mayfield and Paducah. After about 15 miles as I came down a slight hill and started up the next small one I felt the car start to spin and I was going up the road backwards. There wasn't as much snow because it was ice. After trying again with a worse result (full circle) my partner told me she did not want to go any further. I can't really use her exact words but they surely got the message across. So back to Huntington we crept. I had noticed a small hotel when we passed through a little while back and they had one upstairs room available.

39

Well, we got our bags, checked in and looked for the elevator. Oops, only a long steep stairway! Oh, well we were young and in good shape!

By this time the outside temperature was now down in the teens so we hurried up the stair anxious to get in a warm room. I finally found a light cord hanging from a single bulb in the middle of a very sparse room. Once I got the light on and looked for the heat control I found it. It was a sign on the inside of the door that said "If you want heat in the room open the transom!" No heat except for a potbellied stove in the downstairs lobby! That was the night we learned how to snuggle and keep each other warm!

Of course, I called Mom, she was more concerned with our well-being than with all she had to do to cancel and reschedule the party. And we did make it the next day- slowly and carefully. And there was a fine party which allowed me to show off Mickey. They were all impressed!

I doubt that this qualifies as a crossroad but it's fun to remember and be reminded that in spite of my "dumbness" Mickey didn't throw me out!

## Newlyweds at Sewanee

After our very pleasant Paducah visit we made the trip to Sewanee- our new home. Unfortunately, when we got there we found that our apartment in "Fertile Acres" was not yet ready. There was one room in the Sigma Nu House that had been a bedroom during the war years when the house was occupied by a professor and his wife. So we moved in and for a couple of months we lived right above the pool room. I'm not sure who was more distracted – the members or the newlyweds.

Finally, we got settled in our new apartment and began learning how to live together, go to school, work at our jobs and have a great time in a wonderful college environment. In addition to the normal class work I now spent much time leading the Sigma Nu activity, working for Dr. Guerry, managing the intra-mural program and trying to learn to be a good husband. Mickey soon was employed in the alumni office where, among other things, she managed student P.R. releases to home town newspapers. We were two happy and busy people! Life was good! What a fantastic crossroad!

# Chapter 5

# <u>Preparation for a Career</u>

- Beginning to Focus on a Career

- The Final College Year

- An Event From the Previous Spring

- General Shoe Corp

- The Final College Barrier

- Graduation

## Beginning to Focus on a Career

In early 1947 I knew that I was just a year away from graduation and had the need to determine what career directions I would go. My economics major was providing insights into important aspects of how our economy functions and key aspects of business management. But I was a long way from any specific idea of what specific job(s) I should try to find. However, I was beginning to give serious thought to it.

I knew that some form of management was what I liked and for which I had some experience and skill. So I began to think about how I could get better prepared to be considered by top employers. For the first time the concept of a graduate degree (MBA) surfaced. More on this later.

## The Final College Year

My priorities seemed to be something like: Mickey; Classes and study; Sigma Nu; The intra-mural program; Honor Council (I was now chairman); fun and games in our spare time. And the months slipped by.

In the Fall as my last semester started, the question of what I would do after graduation in February 1948 became more and more pressing. My gut feeling was that I should go for the MBA at a quality university and I began to research them. A friend of Mom and Dad's in Nashville had a contact with the Chase Bank in New York and helped me make a strong job contact there since my economics major pointed in that direction. Hi Haynie, another "Eco" major and good friend was having similar thoughts and activity. He had a New York prospect and he had a car! We decided to make the trip – he provided the car. I bought the gas. We headed for New York. Since we would pass through Philadelphia and my graduate school research had highlighted the Wharton School of the University of Pennsylvania I made an interview appointment there.

Hi's New York cousins put us up. My interview with Chase Bank went well. When they saw that I had a minor in Spanish the focus settled on their international program and South/Central America as the target. I left with copious papers to complete and a clear indication that the prospect was promising. That day Witt came up from Fort Dix where he was stationed and we had a fine visit. Hi took a great picture of us atop the Empire State Building.

On the way back to Sewanee Hi was good enough to kill time in Philly while I had my interview at Wharton. The interview was held only 1 block from the University City Science Center where I had my office many years later while I headed the footwear industry trade association. The interview went well. There seemed to be no problem concerning entrance in February '48 once I completed additional papers, got my G.I. Bill clearance and sent the entrance fee.

Hi's interview for law school in New York had also gone well so we headed back to Sewanee in good spirits.

## An Event From the Previous Spring

During the previous spring softball season I was on the Sigma Nu team playing the ATO's. I had gotten a hit and wound up on 3$^{rd}$ base. The game was tied. I was determined to score if I had the chance. One of my teammates got a deep grounder to the infield and I took off for home. George Evans was the ATO catcher. The throw to home got to him while I was about a yard away. I plowed into him as hard as I could go. The ball popped out of his glove and George and I rolled toward the backstop as I crossed the plate. He was mad and wanted to fight. The other players kept us apart. Later that day I searched him out and apologized for the hit. He said "Oh, what the heck, If I had been on third I would have done the same thing!" And we became lifelong good friends. He graduated that semester! Later I found out where he had gone after graduation and you will find out soon. Crossroad? Yep!

When I got back to Sewanee I was surely glad to see Mickey and gave her a full account of all that had gone on and of my inclination to accept the opportunity at Wharton and get the MBA. The Chase situation was appealing but had a lot of negatives - What job? What country? etc. She really wasn't excited about that either. When we paused in that discussion she told me there were a few pieces of mail for me. Among them was a letter from the U.S. Government (G.I. Bill) the gist of which was that in answer to my earlier letter to them asking for clarification of my further G.I. eligibility a mistake had been made. Instead of 2 more years my eligibility would be exhausted upon my graduation from Sewanee in February 1948. There went Wharton!

Another letter was from a company that I had never heard of General Shoe Corporation, Nashville, TN. The letter invited me to come to Nashville for an interview concerning their "Flying Squadron Executive Training Program." A present participant in the program, George Evans, had recommended me! How about that for a complicated crossroad?!

Since Mom and Dad now lived in Nashville we hurried to accept General Shoe's invitation and in late Fall we headed for Nashville for the interview.

## General Shoe Corporation

My interview at Chase Bank was conducted by assistants this and that. You can imagine my surprise at General Shoe to first be interviewed by the Vice President of Industrial Relations (we would now say "Human Resources") Anderson Spickard ; then the Marketing V.P. Matt Wigginton; next the Manufacturing V.P.; Nelson Carmichael and finally the President, Henry Boyd and the Chairman Maxey Jarman. I was impressed! Mr.Jarman and I had a vigorous discussion about economic theories. I was prepared- after all I had been studying that stuff for almost 2 years.

The "Flying Squadron Program" was impressive. The objective - 18 carefully selected graduating veterans to be trained for 18 months in every aspect of this rapidly growing business and then given the opportunity to select, if they could sell themselves to the director, the part of the company they wanted to serve. And as one moved on another was added. And it paid $200 per month (Increased to $250 before I actually started). P.S. George Evans was one of the 18.

It didn't take Mickey and me long to decide that this was what we wanted to do. We accepted and consider it <u>one of the best crossroads of our lives!</u>

### The Final College Barrier

At most colleges the student finishes his last semester classes, gets his grades, adds them up with his previous grades and if they meet the school requirements he passes and gets his degree. Not at Sewanee! Over the years a very powerful torture has been created! It's called the "Comprehensive Exam". What this means is that in your major field you must pass a three hour written exam covering every course taken in your major field. And, as though this isn't punishment enough, you must undergo a two hour oral exam with two major professors covering all of these courses. And, in my case, it was timed just after the Christmas break in 1947.

I was so immersed in study that I can't even remember what Mickey and I did for our first Christmas together. She says, "I don't remember either." How about that for great memories?!

But I can clearly remember January 17, 1948 when I got the word that I passed both exams and would graduate on February 6. What a celebration we had!

### Graduation

Graduation meant a major adjustment in our life. Of course, going to Nashville where Mom and Dad now lived made it easier since we could stay with them for a month or two until I got some paychecks and we could find an apartment that we could afford. I cashed my last $25 war bond for $22.19 which permitted me to rent a small truck to bring our stuff to Nashville. Dad and Mom brought the truck to the graduation. The service was small- only 11 of us (since it was mid-year) but impressive. And then we headed for Nashville with Dad, Mom, Mickey and orphan cat "Duchess" in the front cab and George sitting on a chair in the back with our dog "Duke". We were happy and excited about the new crossroad we were taking. College behind us, career ahead! At 23,George, and 22, Mickey, were ready.

44

# Chapter 6

## <u>General Shoe, Politics and a Growing Family</u>

- Welcome to General Shoe

- Early Days in Nashville- Patricia Maureen Langstaff

- Brother Witt's Wedding

- A Change in my Story Telling  Technique

- A New Decade- The Fifties

- Angela Lynne Langstaff

- The Quetico

- 1952 – Presidential Election

- Massachusetts

- Danville, KY

- Katherine Irene Langstaff

## Welcome to General Shoe

My first days at General Shoe were interesting, impressive and even exciting. The Flying Squadron concept had been explained during my interviews but now I began to see the genius of it. Dr. Joe Ray who was in charge of all of the company training spent a large part of my first day walking me through the training I would undergo for the next 18 months. The objective was to give the trainee a full understanding of the entire process of the company-design, market, manufacture, finance etc. My responsibility was to complete an extensive training manual within 18 months.

When you consider that in the manufacturing area alone I was to learn to actually perform each operation in the production of men's, women's and children's shoes it provided a huge challenge and that was only a start. To mention a few more important categories: designing the product; buying the materials; traveling with the salesmen; working in retail stores; accounting for financial activity; employing, training and managing employees and on and on!! I was somewhat aghast but excited about it.

He then introduced me to those squadron men who were in "The Squadron Room" that day. I was impressed with their quality and their experiences. We would become friendly competitors and partners over the next decades.

Bottom Line - I was, and still am, tremendously impressed with Dr. Ray and the amazing array of training programs he had created to bring this company to the forefront of its industry. And I was also impressed that top management was making the investment to permit this to happen. I concluded that I was with a winner.

For eighteen months I vigorously pursued the program. At the conclusion, I had the chance to decide in what part of the business I wanted to invest my career. But that's for later.

## Early Days in Nashville - Patricia Maureen Langstaff

Mickey and I enthusiastically searched for an apartment of our own. Our budget was no more then $85/month. We still did not have a car so being near a bus line was essential. And within a month or so we also found out that Mickey was pregnant! Great joy/great concern! And I was shifting from job to job and location to location each week as I started to learn the shoe business. How Mickey put up with all of this is hard to imagine. We settled into a nice duplex on Battlefield Dr. and watched and waited for our first child.

On September 17, 1948 early in the morning Mickey started into labor. Since we still had no car we were depending on Dad for transportation. About 6:30 a.m. I called to let him know about the situation and found that he had already left for work but first was going to call on "some customers". (no cell phones in those days).In panic I called Russell Martin who lived nearby and he came to take us to Vanderbilt Hospital. I had also alerted Mickey's doctor. When we arrived at the hospital we could not be admitted until I paid $150 up front. I was not prepared for that and didn't have that much. Good old Russell volunteered to be at the bank when it opened in about an hour and bring the money. Mickey was "about to have the baby in the lobby" so they took her on into a delivery room but kept me hostage in the lobby. Russ came with the money. We moved to a father's waiting room and waited! And waited! Finally the door opens and Dr. Cowan and nurse rolled a carriage in and held up this beautiful little baby girl. What a joy! Patricia Maureen Langstaff just looked around – not crying – as though to say "Well, here I am! Aren't I cute?" Mickey was fine and we were two proud parents. A vast and wonderful crossroad had just been navigated and what a joy it turned out to be!

Soon we moved to another apartment on Belmont Blvd to save money and to be more convenient to the bus line and stores (still no car).

I had been asked by Cecil Wray, a friend of Mom and Dad's to be the Scout Master of the Burton Hills School Troop. Cecil had an extra car and let me use it as a "bribe" to do the scout master job! I enjoyed the job and really enjoyed the car usage!!

One scout story - The youngsters in the troop came from good families, were in one of the better middle schools and were a pleasure to work with. I especially enjoyed our hikes and overnight campouts. Right down my alley! As in any group you find some who stand out from the rest. We had one young man who impressed me a lot. He did his scout work well, was a natural leader among the other boys, had a fine personality, was good at sports etc. However, he started missing a few meetings or being tardy at other times. So one night I asked him to stay a few minutes after the meeting. We discussed my concerns about missed meetings, etc. He explained that he had started taking singing lessons and that some days they conflicted with scout troop activity. I, of course, expressed my viewpoint that scouting and all that goes with it provides a sound foundation for life and I hated to see him lose that great opportunity. In the next 20 years he went on to prove that my viewpoint had some flaws. His name? Pat Boone!


**Brother Witt's Wedding**

In the summer of 1949, brother Witt who was now out of the army and finishing college at Georgia Tech, got a summer job as a counselor at a youth camp in Wisconsin. Before the summer was over he met a beautiful Yankee girl from Chicago who was also a counselor. By the end of the summer Witt and Helen Neumeister were in love. This ultimately brought about a memorable family event. Mom's sister, Madora (Dodie), with husband Wally Bieger lived in Lake Bluff, Illinois on Lake Michigan just north of Chicago. The wedding was held in nearby <u>Lake Forest, Illinois</u> on <u>6/24/50</u>. Mickey, Trish and I traveled with Mom and Dad to the big event.

Helen and Witt's marriage also led to an important development in our life. We were still "carless" and doing our activities by bus, borrowed cars, walking, etc. As a wedding gift the Neumeisters gave Witt and Helen a new car. In an incredible exhibition of brotherly love Witt offered to sell me his old car for $1.00. It was a Buick with several years on it. But it still ran well and to me it looked great. We took the bus to Kingsport, paid our $1.00, and drove back to Nashville in our very first car! (Thanks to Witt and Helen) I can testify that this was a huge crossroad!!

## A Change In the "Crossroads" Storytelling Technique

Up to this point it has been rather easy to remember and describe the crossroads of a comparatively simple life. Now, as I look into the future, life becomes increasingly complex. After much thought I have concluded that I should attempt to look at the crossroads of (1) Our family, (2) My job career, (3) Civic and Religious Activity and (4) Special Events.

I will attempt to keep the narratives in approximately the same time sequence, about 10 year bites.

## A New Decade-The Fifties

So here we are at the start of a new decade. George (25), Mickey (24) and Trish (2)! So much was going on that it's hard to know where to start. So I'll bring you up to date on job career first.

After starting in the General Shoe training program in February 1946 I spent 18 months learning every aspect of a complex business. I learned about customer research, product design, manufacturing men's, women's and children's shoes. We were actually taught to perform every job in the factory. And we had to personally make a pair of shoes in each category for our family's use. Then we traveled with salesmen presenting their products for sale to independent retailers. We worked in General Shoe retail stores; warehouses; in house operations such as accounting, buying, personnel, etc. In other words "We did it all!" And we were evaluated on our performance.

Finally, at the conclusion of my 18 months (September 1949) I had the opportunity to select the part of the business I wanted to work in. And then it was my responsibility to sell the manager of that operation on finding a job in his organization for me.

For me the decision was easy. I liked manufacturing! Somehow I knew from my first week in a factory that I was right for it and it was right for me! Most of my training partners thought I was nuts! Most wanted retail, marketing, purchasing, etc.

Eli White (one of the most effective executives that I ever encountered) was General Manager of Women's Manufacturing and, of course, I had trained in several of his plants. So I asked for an opportunity to see him. We hit it off great but he had no openings in any of his plants. However, he could put me in a training role in a new experimental operation called "The Model Plant" which was in a part of the Main St. factory in Nashville. The Model Plant's purpose was to quickly turn a designer's concept of a new style into a real marketable sample for use in fashion presentations, etc.

Well, that wasn't what I had in mind but it was in Nashville and Henry Wills, a veritable manufacturing genius, was in charge of it. So I accepted and soon started to work. How fortunate that was! Talk about a crossroad!

In a short period of time Henry Wills turned me from an apprentice into a real shoemaker. And, not only that, but he taught me (a college graduate, etc.) how to effectively manage and motivate an employee team of mostly women and a few men from backgrounds far different from mine. Before long the model plant was converted into a full women's shoe plant (9<sup>th</sup> Ave. plant) and I was the manager of the fitting room staffed by some 100 women at sewing and related machines assembling and stitching the uppers of women's high heeled shoes. Raymond Wilson (the machinist) and I were the only men in sight!

For some 2 ½ years I ran this department. I learned so much about managing people, making shoes, planning factory workloads and schedules, etc. that it's hard to describe. It was good for me!

During 1950-1951 Several interesting and /or important events occurred:

- Our first house was purchased-

  After renting 3 different homes in Nashville we finally decided to buy a modest home on Sharon-dale Court. It was expensive ($9,000) but we were able to afford it. And what a joy that was!

- On Sharondale Court we became good friends with 2 couples Hoppie and Nancy Smith, Harold and Mary Anna West who together with Dot and Ernie Moench became the nucleus of a monthly Bridge Group that continued for 60 years. When the Smiths left Nashville, Creed and Catherine Black (my old debate partner) replaced them until they left town and then Val (Mike) and Betty Sanford joined us.

- In January of 1951 Nashville experienced a blizzard with the greatest snow accumulation in history. I walked 2 blocks in 18" of snow to Hillsboro Rd. at about 6:00 A.M. to catch the bus to the plant only to find not one set of tire tracks on this major road. I finally caught a ride in a pickup truck with chains and reached the plant about 9:30 A.M. Normal opening was at 7:00 A.M. No one else had arrived! Our son in law, George Stockman, was born during the big blizzard!

- Most important of all - In late 1950 <u>Mickey was pregnant</u> with a due date of late May 1951. Let me tell you about the arrival of Angela Lynne Langstaff.

### Angela Lynne Langstaff

About September 1950 we discovered with joy that Mickey was expecting again. All went along well until spring of 1951 when she started bleeding. Dr. Cowan and his staff did all they could to identify and correct the problem. As the bleeding continued it became more and more likely that the pregnancy would have to be terminated if the bleeding did not stop soon in order to protect Mickey. The Easter weekend was just ahead and the doctors concluded that if the bleeding had not stopped by the Monday after Easter the pregnancy would have to be terminated. Our prayers and those of family and friends were constant.

On Good Friday there was a reduction of the bleeding and by Easter Day it stopped!! I believed that our prayers were answered!

On May 14, 1951 Angela Lynne Langstaff entered our lives. As we discussed names her nurse said "Angels intervened. She should be named for them". Voila! Angela! And what a joy Angela Lynne has been to her parents, her family and her many friends! (Shortly afterward Mickey's problem was corrected by removal of her left kidney which had apparently been faulty from birth. Thankfully she has done well ever since.)

This whole episode was not only a fantastic and positive crossroad but a true blessing from the Lord!

### The Quetico

Brother Quint was in his program to become a family doctor. He had completed Johns Hopkins for his B.S. Degree, Duke University for his M.D. and was now in residency at the University Of Michigan Hospital. There he met Tom who lived in the area and was familiar with a very special canoeing area in Canada called "The Quetico". He sold Quint on the concept of a two canoe one week trip into the Quetico to camp, fish, etc. Quint immediately enlisted his canoeing brothers for the big adventure. We went and it was an important "fun crossroad" for me, my sons-in-law, my grandsons, and a daughter. I fell in love with the area and later, when they were 14, brought each grandson and his Dad for a week in the Quetico. Kathy went on Greg's trip and she was a real trooper! Brother Witt went with us on Sam's trip when Charles, his dad and daughter Trish's husband, had a business conflict. Later Charles and I took a twosome trip so he could see that great place. It was the best thing I could ever have done to develop a wonderful relationship with them.

## 1952 - Presidential Election

1952 contained life and career changing crossroads that I could never have foreseen. Even after completing the Flying Squadron training, the company offered an impressive assortment of additional training opportunities. One was the opportunity to participate in "Mr. Jarman's Lunch Group". Maxey Jarman was our C.E.O. and the son of one of the company founders. He was devoted to the concept of careful selection of young executives and of providing well-crafted training opportunities to keep them growing in management skills.

His once a month "Lunch Group" was his way of getting better acquainted with them and testing their growing management skills and understanding. He would visit casually for a while and then throw out a controversial subject for discussion. He was not gentle in challenging your positions. But he surely made you think carefully about your viewpoints. I was fortunate to be invited to several lunches.

In the spring of 1952 I attended one and the issue for discussion was the approaching Presidential Election with special emphasis on the battle within the Republican Party between the "Taft Republicans" and the "Eisenhower Republicans". It was a feisty discussion!

A few days later, a Saturday afternoon, I was cutting grass in the backyard at Sharondale Court. Mickey came rushing out of the back door, stopped me and said "Hurry, Mr. Jarman is on the phone." Well, of course, I stopped and went in to the phone. When I answered a voice said "George, this is Maxey" and, thinking it was one of my buddies giving me a hard time, I said "Yeah, and my name is Abraham Lincoln"

And then he assured me it was really Maxey. He then went on to say that he had been impressed with my comments at last week's lunch and with my strong support for Gen. Eisenhower as opposed to Senator Taft (Ohio) in their campaign to become the Republican Candidate for President. Mr. Jarman was a strong Ike supporter he said. It had not been obvious during the lunch.

His message to me was that he wanted me to chair the "Ike" campaign in Middle Tennessee leading up to the Nominating Convention in Chicago. I was shocked! And clamored something like "But, Mr. Jarman. I couldn't possibly find the time. I have to be at the plant by 6:00 A.M. and rarely get home before 6:30 at night" and he said "Not to worry. I will discuss this with Eli (White) and we'll work it out. Just come to my office about 10:00 Monday and we'll talk about all of this."

And guess what! By 8:00 A.M. Monday morning Frank Pedigo, one of my favorite Assistant Department Managers, arrived from the McMinnville Plant to sub for me. And at 10:00 A.M. I was in the chairman's office being briefed by him and several others on how to become a Politician.

To condense a long story, all summer and into the fall I worked organizing Political activities, Rallies, Speeches, The Republican Convention, running for the Republican State Executive Committee, negotiating with the Taft element after Ike won the nomination to form a joint Middle Tennessee Campaign Committee for the national elections. I became Middle Tennessee Co- campaign Manager together with a Taft Supporter for Eisenhower-Nixon in Middle Tennessee. I worked my fanny off. The result - the state went for Ike. Middle Tennessee went Democrat but with the narrowest margins ever. I won for the State Republican Executive Committee. Mickey was a real trooper to put up with all of this and handled our children and home in a great way.

With great relief and joy I returned to the plant. Frank remained as my assistant. And then about a couple of weeks after the election Eli White asked me to come over to his office. Oh, gosh, what now?

## Massachusetts

Eli explained that the Massachusetts company, Klevin Shoe, which General Shoe had recently purchased, needed help in modernizing its manufacturing system and he wanted me to move there and help them install our "Clear Channel System". Klevin operated with some 40 days in process while our southern plants required only 6 days. It was a matter of preplanning and day by day oversight. Should be an easy transition! Hah!

And so I headed for Spencer, Massachusetts on December 1 and set about evaluating their systems and searching for a place for us to live when we moved after January 1.

The three weeks before Christmas went well. I found a nice furnished home in Holden for rent until the next summer. A bright young man (son of the superintendent) was assigned to me and we started to evaluate what needed to be done.

Following a short trip home for Christmas Mickey and I packed up the car and the two girls and set out driving to Massachusetts. The trip was OK and we got settled in our new home in Holden only some 20 miles from Spencer. And I plunged into the business of creating a system which could accomplish our agreed target of 10 days in process.

Before long we learned about New England winters. During a night in January it snowed about 18 inches. I backed out of the driveway at 6:00 A.M. (we lived on a modest hill). About 8:00 A.M. I got back even with our driveway. And that's when I learned about snow tires. After help from a local dealer I got outfitted with the snow tires and a set of chains. I made it to the plant by noon. Those Yankees sure had fun kidding the rebel!!

As we refined the new factory system and trained the managers and employees in its use, we saw the in-process time beginning to drop. I could also sense a frustration on the part of the former owner, Harry Bass, over some of the restrictions which the system imposed. However we moved steadily on and by April were operating on 10 days in process.

In the meantime (and probably due to those very cold nights) Mickey was pregnant again. I had only agreed to stay 6 months and we wanted very much to get back to her Nashville doctors (especially considering what she had experienced before). Eli was very understanding. My team was operating smoothly. In process held steady at 10 days. So on June 1 we said our goodbyes and headed back south.

After a few weeks in the home office I was promoted to Assistant Superintendent of the Danville, KY Plant. So off we went again.

P.S. After 6 months the in process time at the Klevin Plant was back to over 40 days. Another lesson learned- unless the natives are enthusiastic about new systems, techniques, etc. it is very hard to make the "new" successful.

## Danville, Kentucky

What a terrific town Danville is. We settled in easily with a pleasant house on Boyd Ave. surrounded by very friendly neighbors with young children and an elementary school nearby. I loved my new job! Finally I was in a position to participate in the management of an entire factory - all aspects. And for 4 years we reveled in all aspects of Danville – job, social life, developing family, church, etc. We lived near a fine small lake and I had many opportunities to polish my fly fishing skills.

On several occasions we had visits from senior General Shoe executives and sometimes I was their tour director. Eli White came regularly and on one occasion Nelson Carmichael, director of all footwear manufacturing, came for a full day visit and joined our department manager's meeting. He and I discussed many things on his tour through the factory. I had no idea then how important this visit would be to my future.

One of the saddest days of my life occurred while we were in Danville. My cousin Tommy Langstaff, then a captain in the Air Force, came by to visit us in Holden, Massachusetts when he was in transit from a tour in Korea to his new assignment in England. We had a great time getting up to date on what had been going on in our lives. He was now married (Anna Gail). All wars were over for him and he was looking forward to a chance for them to see Europe.

And then in the fall of 1953 I received a dreadful message. "On a high altitude training mission over England Tom's oxygen system failed. He lost consciousness, crashed and was killed." The best friend I ever had was gone forever.

When his funeral was held in Paducah I drove from Danville at night to be there. During that drive I had an experience that is hard to explain. Tommy was with me in the car and we relived our many great times together from earliest days until his visit to Holden. I know that is not possible but it was very real for me. At the funeral the next day I gave Anna Gail (who was now expecting their child) Tommy's West Point cuff link which I had gotten from him in our exchange at mid-field following that Army-Navy game when he was at West Point and I was at Annapolis. His picture, drawn by brother Witt, hangs over my desk at home. I often visit his grave in Paducah. We were not just cousins of the same age but lifelong best friends. And speaking for best friend cousins, this is a good time to tell you about Sue Langstaff Bowman my great "Lady Cousin" friend. She is the daughter of my Dad's twin brother, Sam. We are almost exactly the same age, therefore, were in the same classes in grade school through high school. She always out performed me in grades. (Salutatorian in junior high and high school) She was my strong supporter and most effective (and gentle) critic. When I started dating she kept me posted on how I was doing. ☺

To me she is like my sister and we still stay in touch although she and her husband, Bill (now deceased) settled in West Virginia and raised their fine family there.

## Katherine Irene Langstaff

During the early months in Danville Mickey's pregnancy moved along normally but we missed the care she had received from Nashville's strong medical community - especially Dr. Cowan. So she kept him informed and we decided that after the seventh month she should come back to Nashville with Trish and Lynne, stay with Mom and Dad and be under Dr. Cowan's care. And the transfer was made.

It took about 5 hours to get from Danville to Nashville so our plan was that when Mickey had her first labor pain Dad would call me and I would start driving. Dad would then take Mickey to the hospital. Mom would take care of Trish and Lynne. I would arrive in time for the birth and all would be well!

At the plant we were in the process of setting up a new raw material purchasing and supply system and I was working long hours to get it perfected. On the critical day I finally got home and into bed about midnight. I was sound asleep and heard nothing! About 2:00 A.M. Uncle Witt, at Dad's request, started calling me to tell me that the labor had started and Dad was taking Mickey to the hospital. About 5:00 A.M. I heard the phone, got the message and in a panic loaded up and started for Nashville. I probably broke lots of speed limits and skidded into the hospital parking lot about 10:00 A.M. When I got to Mickey's room there she was but no baby. The baby had arrived and Mickey was doing well. So I rushed to the room where the new babies were displayed. There was our new daughter Katherine Irene Langstaff!  And when the nurse brought her over to me "Kathy" looked at her Daddy as though to say "Where in the_____ have you

54

been?!" She forgave me as did Mickey. Our treasured family was now complete - Mickey and George plus Trish, Lynne and Kathy! A triple crossroad in my life! And very positive!

When Mickey had recovered sufficiently we all came back home to Danville. And there we watched our little family begin its fascinating development.

# Chapter 7

## Back to Nashville

- A Disappointment
- Nelson Carmichael
- Back To The Family

## A Disappointment

As I pursued my role of Assistant Superintendent my whole focus was on preparing myself to become a superintendent and have my own factory to manage. By 1956 I felt that I was ready. A new women's shoe factory was under construction in Smithville, Tennessee and I really hoped it would be mine. About the time the construction was almost complete, Eli White (The General Manager of Women's Manufacturing) visited Danville and paged me to come to the office. I was sure that he would tell me that I was to be the new superintendent of the Smithville Plant. What a disappointment when he told me Brandon Edmonson was to get the job. To be honest, Brandon had more experience and was better prepared, but it hurt anyway. Eli went on to say that I was being transferred to Nashville to serve as Assistant Superintendent of the Charlotte Ave. women's dress shoe plant. It was to broaden my experience etc. There was a nice salary increase so we prepared to return to Nashville. While we were in Danville we had sold the house on Sharondale Court (which we had rented while we were in Danville) so we searched for a place to rent. And we found one fairly close to Mom and Dad and St. George's Episcopal Church.

The Charlotte Ave plant was an expansion of the 9$^{th}$ Ave. plant where I had managed the fitting department for several years so I felt right at home. But I wasn't there long. After a few weeks I was asked to come to Nelson Carmichael's office in the corporate offices downtown. He explained that after his visit with me in Danville he had decided to invite me to be one of his Administrative Assistants. What a surprise and what excitement! The company then operated over 30 factories with more coming and I was going to be an assistant to the Vice President in charge of all that! Holy mackerel! I had never considered such a move. I was elated! And, in time, it turned out to be one of the most important crossroads of my business career.

## Nelson Carmichael

Nelson Carmichael was an incredible role model. He grew up in Laurel, Mississippi, graduated from Western Kentucky University in accounting, and joined the young General Shoe Corporation in the accounting and control area. His rise in the company was meteoric. When I joined the company in 1948 he was already a Vice President, a Board Member, and a member of the Executive Committee. And I soon began to understand why.

His reputation told me he was a prodigious worker; a tough boss who demanded results from his team; a man who expected his executives to be of high moral character; who was a committed Christian himself, was a strong family man, and a strong leader in his church. He was known to be fair in his evaluations of his associates. I liked what I heard. Would it prove to be accurate?!

It didn't take long to see that this reputation was well earned. His normal work day was 5:45 A.M. to 6:00 P.M. Since I was accustomed to 6:00 A.M. to 6:00 P.M. the minor adjustment was easy. Jim Cheek, his senior Administrative Assistant (and to whom I reported) occupied an adjacent office to Carmichael and my desk was in the hall outside their doors. Within a short time I started assuming the responsibility for several key functions of the manufacturing group such as: (1) Coordination of all activities concerning building new plants- location, design, construction oversight, etc.,(2) Manufacturing Staff (10-15 highly skilled experts in all aspects of manufacturing who acted as consultants to the factories (3) Machine Storage and acquisition - the department that managed our machinery requirements for all plants, etc. And, of course, I was also called on constantly by Carmichael and Cheek for many other assignments. Man! Did I ever begin to get a whole new vision of what it took to run an operation of 30+ factories, warehouses, shipping departments, purchasing, etc.

Mr. Carmichael was a terrific mentor, coach, critic, and friend. Jim Cheek became a lifelong friend and tennis playing buddy. For three years I worked in this role and began to really understand complex management. I loved it!

And then one day Mr. Carmichael called me in and said " Ben would like for you to come up and see him" (Ben Wiliingham was President of General Shoe - soon to be renamed " Genesco") Oh, my gosh, what have I done now?! More on this later.

## Back To the Family

After we returned to Nashville and were settled in a rental home in The Highlands we started looking for a home to purchase. Within a short time we found one only a few blocks away. We liked it a lot but the down payment was more than we had so we had to pass. That weekend Gayle and Virginia Taylor from Paducah were visiting with Mom and Dad. Mom brought Virginia by to see us and our three daughters. As we sat around chatting Mom asked what happened on the house we had been looking at. I explained that we had passed on it and why. Virginia wanted to know how much the down payment was. When I told her she took out her checkbook, wrote me a check for the amount and said "You can just pay me back when you can!"

And we bought this nice home on Brookfield Drive. It took two years to pay her back and when I tried to pay her interest she wouldn't accept it so we sent it as a contribution to Grace Church in Paducah. Now how about that for good friends!

Their son, Tim, had been one of my baby sitting customers many years before. He is now (2012) an Associate Priest at our church, St. George's Episcopal, in Nashville. Gayle and Virginia had helped me obtain the Annapolis appointment. Small world! We settled happily into our new home.

# Chapter 8

## <u>George The Spy</u>

- A visit with President Willingham

- Family update

- Most challenging assignment of my business career to date

- Acquiring the team

- Creating the strategy

### A Visit with President Ben Willingham

With some trepidation I went from the 9<sup>th</sup> to the 12<sup>th</sup> floor in the Genesco building and entered the President's office. I had been there once years before when I was interviewed by then President Henry Boyd (now deceased) for the Flying Squadron Training Program.

As our discussion unfolded it was clear that the purpose was to find out what I knew about Williams Manufacturing Company of Portsmouth, Ohio. Well, I knew that they dominated the low price $3-5 Women's shoe business. Rumor had it that they had developed a manufacturing system that was far ahead of anyone else, and that was about all I knew.

Much to my shock Mr. Willingham then said something like – "Well, George I want you to study everything about Williams and determine what we would have to do to compete with them. I have arranged with Nelson for you to report to me while you undertake this project. It's up to you to determine how you approach your assignment. All Genesco doors are open to your inquiries. Let me know what you need in order to get the job done. "

I stumbled back to my desk and must have sat there in a trance. Nelson walked by, gave a big laugh, patted me on the back and said something like – "Well, I told Ben that you were getting a little bored and needed a challenge. How did I do? " At that time I had no concept as to what an enormous and important crossroad this would be for me.

### Family Update

Since returning to Nashville our family was a happy bunch! "Gram and Granddaddy" were nearby and very involved with "The girls". The Irion cousins lived only a couple of blocks from Gram and Granddaddy so family get togethers were frequent. Trish and Lynne were attending Parmer Elementary School nearby and at 4 years old Kathy started Kindergarten at St. George's. Trish had her first school year at Maple Ave Grammer School in Danville.

Mickey was one busy lady taking care of our girls, managing the household, putting up with her husband's very demanding work requirements, ultimately serving on P.T.A. Boards, driving hookups (Dottie Moench taught her to drive when we lived on Sharondale Court) and being a great wife!

## And Now Comes the Most Challenging Assignment of My Business Career to Date

After thinking about the "Williams assignment" for a day or so I concluded that my first step should be to obtain all information that I could from (1) Genesco Executives who knew anything about them (2) Our mutual suppliers of raw materials, shoe machinery, financial services (3) Footwear News writers and articles etc. Footwear News was the trade paper covering the broad footwear industry. And so I set to work.

To make a complex story short I will just say that within a month I accumulated a lot of information. But I felt a lot like a doctor might feel if asked to diagnose an ill patient with only input from acquaintances of the patient and no chance to observe the patient first hand.

At Genesco we maintained an "open door policy" and were pleased to have visits from competitors, customers, suppliers, etc. It was our feeling that we learned as much from them as they did from us. So I thought - "Why don't I call Forest (Frosty) Williams (their president) and ask if I could visit their plant." One key element of their manufacturing success seemed to be the incredible computer supported conveyor system which produced faster and cheaper results than anyone else in the industry. With the manufacturing experience I had, a walk through their plant should let me see how much better they were and why.

So I called Mr. Williams and asked for an opportunity to visit Williams. We had a nice conversation and he agreed for me to visit and we set a date the next week. At Genesco I was operating on my own so no one knew my plans except that I had been talking to many people about Williams.

I arrived mid-afternoon the day before my appointment with Mr. Williams, checked in a local motel and took a drive around the area. The Williams company was impressive – Large 3 story building across the street from a last manufacturing factory with which we did a lot of business. Lasts are the form around which the shoe is shaped prior to attaching the sole. I had a nice dinner at a local restaurant and hit the sack.

The next morning I arrived at Williams 5 minutes before my scheduled appointment, checked in with the receptionist and took a seat in the lobby. Shortly Mr. Williams arrived, introduced himself and took a seat. After some small talk I explained, at his request, my background with Genesco. It's important to understand that at the time Genesco was vastly bigger and more complex than Williams - probably about 15-1. I explained how impressed the industry was with Williams and how I was looking forward to my visit and the opportunity to exchange ideas.

After about 30 minutes of conversation it was apparent that the lobby was all that I was going to see of Williams Mfg Co. He thanked me for coming and that was that!

Now what?! I was in Portsmouth. A large supplier of lasts to Genesco was right there. What the heck, I'll visit them and see what they can tell me about Williams. I did! They did! And I began to accumulate significant information. On a walk through the last plant I discovered that windows on their upper floor looked directly into Williams's windows and provided a perfect look at their factory conveyor. I asked for permission to sit at the window for a while. No problem! I left, came back with a new pair of binoculars and spent the rest of the day seated at the windows with the binoculars, a stop watch and a notebook.

After the work day I walked around the Williams Plant and found some discarded "tickets" which in a shoe factory define materials to be used and the operations to be performed. I also noticed that many of the workers were congregated at a bar just about a block away. I went to have a beer! (I don't drink but pantomimed very well) Before long we had some vigorous discussions about the plant – systems, conveyor, in process times, quality control and on and on. It proved to be a highly successful day!

My next focus was on Williams' sales and marketing activity and this proved to be very rewarding. In essence, their strategy was to build short product lines of carefully market tested styles, be prepared to deliver orders as soon as the salesmen hit the road each season, price to permit a favorable mark up for the retailers and $2.95 to $4.95 retail price points for the consumer. Their marketing director, Bob Holzemer, had created a simple but powerful training program for a highly qualified sales force. All reports that I received confirmed the excellence or their whole approach. (Bob later became an important Genesco Executive.)

Bottom Line- I spent some time digesting my findings and evaluating our potential to compete head to head with Williams. The more I studied it, the more certain I was that we could compete provided senior management endorsed some key steps.

1. A completely new operating division should be formed that included both the manufacturing and marketing functions under the new division president.
2. One of Genesco's new Mississippi factories should be assigned to the new division These were our lowest cost factories.
3. An Independent shipping facility should be assigned or created for the new operation

4. The division manager should be selected from within and given the authority to build his staff to include heads of line building, manufacturing, sales, etc.

When I was ready to talk, Mr. Willingham invited me to make my presentation to Genesco's Executive Committee. Oh, my gosh! I expected only Willingham.

My total report was contained in a notebook more than one inch thick and we talked about it for some 3 hours.

Finally, the committee endorsed the concept of moving ahead as soon as practicable. I was asked to provide a list of Genesco Executives who were capable of managing this division. I gave a list of four names with my name last.

A few days later Ben's secretary called to set up a meeting in his office the next day. To say that I was somewhat nervous about the meeting would be a considerable understatement. When I arrived for the meeting I was surprised to see Eli White and DeVaughn Woods, Corporate Controller, as well as Mr. Willingham. Eli, you will remember was General Manager of Women's manufacturing. I had worked in his organization for several years and we had a strong, positive relationship. DeVaughn I knew well through some social contacts.

Ben led the discussion outlining the Executive Committee decision on my report. He was quite complimentary of the work I had done. This let me relax a little.

Essentially, my report had been accepted. The Fulton, Mississippi Factory would be the plant for the new division. Eli would work with the new division manager in phasing in the new production while maintaining sufficient production from current sources to keep the plant operating smoothly.

The new shipping location would be authorized and it would be up to the new division to obtain space and set it up.

The new Division Manager would report to DeVaughn Woods since it would be so different from other company units. This would be a stand-alone business just like an entrepreneur setting up a new business from scratch. DeVaughn's financial savvy would be essential to the new experiment.

And now the big question- who was going to run this new child? They held this answer to the last and then congratulated me on my new job - President of "XYZ" Shoe Company! I was excited but also overwhelmed at the scope of the new challenge.

This was a crossroad that carried with it an enormous requirement for hard work, dedication, sound judgment, and good luck.

If I were to detail all that went into creating Charm Step Shoe Company it would require a huge volume. So, I will just touch the high points.

- Acquiring the necessary management team
    - <u>Operations Manager</u> – Creating balanced assortments of fashion right women's shoes and servicing customers- Bob Richter
    - <u>Sales Management </u>- Designing geographic sales territories and hiring experienced salesmen to present and sell our product – Bob Bloxton
    - <u>Manufacturing Management</u> – Converting the current management team to the new Charm Step Direction and obtaining their expertise in reaching our goals – Richard McGlohn
- Creating a strategy for attacking the U.S. Market step by step
    - Focused first on 11 territories in the Southeast with gradual expansion until full national coverage- Langstaff, Bloxton, Richter
- Product Identity
    - Selection of brand name. After much consideration we chose "Charm Step"
    - Developed point of sale promotional material

Charm Step was ready for its first selling season in the fall of 1959 with a spring 1960 line. The long period spent in getting all the issues described above had been well handled by the new management team.

Operations Director (Product and customer Service) - Bob Richter

Sales Manager – Bob Bloxton

Manufacturing Manager – Richard McGlohn

66

Now it was time for our first sales meeting at which we would present the new line to our 11 man sales force; brief them on many sales oriented issues and, hopefully, send them out with enthusiasm to present and sell our new Charm Step line.

I had never been to a sales meeting much less chaired one so as I walked the two blocks from my office to the hotel where our meeting would be held I was truly nervous. Then I glanced up at the sky and for the first time in my life I saw a magnificent double rainbow. To me that was a special event promising good things ahead for Charm Step.

And led by gifted salesmen, Howard Johnson and Jim Harper the sales performance was excellent - the double rainbow was right!

Charm Step grew rapidly and never lost money except for our first 6 months before we sold and shipped any product. I continued to lead Charm Step for three years. DeVaughn Woods turned out to be an ideal "Boss". He did not try to "run" things but to be a skilled sounding board for me and to act more as a consultant than a "Boss". In other words, he gave me a free hand unless I asked for his input - a terrific man to work with.

Charm Step expanded from the initial "Southern sector strategy" to full national sales coverage over the next 3 years. Our profit performance was excellent. The management team became more and more capable and I was having a ball learning more and more about sales and marketing which had not been my strong points. Two of our managers Bob Richter and Phil Ponder were doing excellent work on product, internal systems, communications, etc. We were moving on!

# Chapter 9

## First Steps On The Corporate Ladder and Family Activities

- And Then I Got Another Call

- Was This a Crossroad?

- Community Involvement

- Update of The Family Activities

- Family Vacations

### And Then I Got Another Call

Nelson Carmichael was not only going to be Director of Footwear Manufacturing but was being promoted to also head Footwear Marketing. He wanted me to become his Marketing Assistant and gradually assume responsibility for the various Genesco Footwear sales divisions.

Again I was taken aback since my marketing training was limited to an M.I.T. – Marketing Strategy and Tactics Course in the first year of Charm Step (1959). But they had plans to help on that. And I did feel that Bob Richter, supported by members of the Charm Step Team and still reporting to me, could do the Charm Step job.

### Was This a Crossroad?

I now admit that I viewed this with some trepidation! Here I was really having fun with a baby I had created from scratch! I loved what I was doing! I was proud of our progress - our team. And yet, what a fantastic opportunity to broaden my knowledge and skills! And, of course, it would improve things financially and offer a tremendous future opportunity. So, thank you, Mr. Carmichael, when do I start? ☺ Yep! It was a huge crossroad! Much more on this later!

### Community Involvement

When we returned to Nashville in 1956 we started a "Rest of life" relationship with *St. George's Episcopal Church* which was a spinoff from downtown Christ Church. Mom and Dad went there and we went prior to our moves away from Nashville. St. George's was much closer. Many of our younger friends went there. It had a terrific Kindergarten.

Mickey and I soon were teaching a high school Sunday School class. Our girls loved all the young people activities- especially the youth choir. I soon was serving my first term on the Vestry (A Vestry operates like a Lay Board of Directors in partnership with the Rector.) I later served another 4 terms with 3 as Senior Warden.

I also served as a board member of Junior Achievement where several years earlier I had been an advisor to one of the "companies." Genesco was very supportive of participation by its executives in community activities. Over the years I had opportunities to also serve on the boards of United Funds of Nashville, Nashville Mental Health Association (President), University of the South (Trustee), etc.

As I grew into the role of Marketing Director for Genesco Footwear I plunged into the activities of the Marketing Committee of the Footwear Industries of America (F.I.A) ultimately chairing the Marketing Committee and the trade show of the industry.

My marketing education was enhanced by courses at the University Of Michigan, American Manufacturers Association, Sarnoff Speech Dynamics, etc.

Now, whether I can call any of these "crossroads" is a good question. I'm not sure. I do know that the more I became involved in such activities the more confidence I had in my ability to organize and manage complex activities and diverse personalities. Maybe I should see them as "launching ramps for the future."

## Update of the Family Activities (1963)

Before we launch into more business activity I have to brag a little about our growing family. Trish – 15, Lynne- 12 and Kathy - 10. They were true individuals – very different in interests, ability and accomplishments. And much to our joy they got along well together.

Trish - Was already showing significant musical ability. My Dad who loved to play the ukulele and sing probably inspired the interest. I will never forget the day that Mickey and I went to a Hillsboro High Talent Contest not knowing that Trish would be one of the contestants. We were enjoying the sequence of performers and then to our shock out comes Trish all dressed up with her guitar! I almost swooned! She did a great job with her playing and singing. We were so proud! (Remember that...later in college at Birmingham – Southern she would be the lead singer in a wonderful group - The Hilltop Singers - which spent two summers at Gatlinburg performing for the tourists)

Lynne - Was our quiet and studious daughter who inherited my mother's wonderful way with people. She loved people and they loved her. Her teachers thought she was a gift from Heaven. And when differences broke out between "The Sisters" she was the peace maker. If we had possessed a crystal ball we could probably have been able to see what a great elementary school teacher she would become. She loved it and at this writing is still providing a great start for youngsters in K – 5th grades. Lynne received her B.A. degree from Birmingham-Southern and her Master's Degree in Reading from University of Alabama-Birmingham.

Kathy- Was not a scholar. She was our athlete! Now, she did OK with the books but her real love was sports. All three daughters were swimmers and swam for our nearby swimming club but Kathy liked basketball. As soon as she reached high school she was a star. As a left hander she was a great defensive player. At that time girls played half court. Left handed offensive players on opposing teams hated her because she could anticipate their moves. She won many awards!

As a family we did many things together. One of our best decisions was that each year we would plan a two week vacation trip – the five of us – to a different part of our country so that the girls (and we) would develop a better understanding of the U.S.A., its history, its geography, its people, etc. And we did a pretty good job of it.

It would take too many pages and too much detail to tell everything about the trips and to present them in time sequence. So I am going to do it all at once here and at least give the reader an overview of what we achieved.

## Family Vacations

At the beginning I want you to know that I consider the "Family Vacation Decision" to be a very important family crossroad! It created family relationships that remain solid and meaningful to this day.

Vacations scheduled and completed:

- California- out the southern way – back the middle way, Mickey's brother and family in L.A.

- Wisconsin- Chicago (Beiger Family in Lake Bluff, IL)

- Florida Pan Handle ( Martin's and Destin)

- South Carolina ( Columbia and The Coast) Mickey's Family

- North Carolina, Virginia, Washington, DC

- New York (World's Fair), Pennsylvania

- Mississippi ( Charm Step Employees)

- * New York - The City – Individually with Mom and Dad

- *Western Europe – Grand tour ( Italy, Switzerland, Germany, France and England)

- Many visits to South Carolina and Kentucky Families

  *- By air – all the rest by car

Every trip has its stories. Whether funny, sad, frustrating or disappointing we remember them as "Family specials". But I must describe a few☺!

Packing up – 2-3 weeks, 5 people, 1 station wagon with a luggage carrier on top and one packer! How it was done I'm not sure. I do know that the girls could not observe because sometimes the language was not lady like.

Window seats - Strict rotation for 3 daughters in the back seat so each had equal time at windows. Sometimes we packed for the rear facing back seats to be used so the girls could flirt with the truck drivers and produce horn toots.

Refreshments - Dairy Queens were in big demand during the long afternoons and the "Three person nagging" to stop at one was a challenge. So we developed a system- after 3:00 P.M. each travel day if they could develop new, pleading words and sing them in acceptable 3 part harmony we would stop at the next opportunity. We got some surprising results!

Historic places and signs - Being a Civil War buff Old Dad tended to stop and read the historic signs (Every one! Trish says) when we drove through significant places. When we arrived at Gettysburg all signs were properly absorbed plus old Dad's battlefield maps. At the bottom of Shy's Hill the four person attack team was drawn up at the bottom and four rebels charged up the hill in memory of Pickett's Charge.

Rebels in Washington D.C. – After a full day of trudging over important sites in North Carolina and Virginia we finally arrived at our fancy hotel in downtown Washington D.C. about 9:00 P.M. There was a formal dinner of some sort in progress. As our bedraggled bunch waited for the elevator the door opened and several formally dressed couples disembarked to find Kathy taking off her sandals and dumping sand and stickers on the floor!

The proposal - Italy was a fascinating place for the girls to see. Mickey and I had been there before so we felt very comfortable about what we would experience. We had missed our plane connection from Rome to Naples and had to take the train. Across the aisle from us was a group of young Italian soldiers and before long they started flirting with the girls. Mickey and I were having fun watching. Before long one of the young men named Rafaele (probably about 20) who had been talking with Kathy came over to me, points at Kathy and starts to sing "Here comes the bride." We never let her forget it!

The Piazza - After a day of sightseeing in Florence and a nice dinner the girls wanted to go down to a nearby Piazza and see a little of Florence at night. So away they went. The old folks stayed behind. In about an hour they came rushing in the door laughing and blushing! It seems the Italian boys in the Piazza liked their looks, came over to flirt and then pinched them on their bottoms!! Welcome to Italy!!

Merry Old England- England looked very good to our gang after our almost three weeks on the continent. We could understand almost everyone. And Jackie and Tuffy Irion lived just outside London. (LT. Col Irion was a military attaché at the U.S. Embassy and is my first cousin.) They had invited us to dinner that first night and we caught the train with enthusiasm. We all knew that Tuffy is a great cook and could hardly wait after the mishmash of food we had experienced on the continent. We were not disappointed. It was great! The girls still talk about it as a highlight of the trip. They say that the lasagna was the best they ever tasted.

# Chapter 10

## A Look Back and The Devil's Roller Coaster

- Twenty Three Incredible Years

- My New Assignment

- My Dad

- 6001 Andover Drive

- The Devil's Roller Coaster

    - Frank Jarman

    - The Search – Jack Hanigan

## Twenty Three Incredible Years  1963 – 1986

From a business standpoint, and in retrospect, this period covers my evolution from a  successful small business  manager to senior level manager of many diverse and challenging businesses including some 46 factories, 1200 retail stores, marketing companies, all the infrastructure necessary to support them and also the many human resource issues which needed to be handled constantly.

One of the most challenging aspects of this was learning to cope with corporate leadership with which I was often at issue. Fortunately or unfortunately this led to some nasty disagreements which presented very complicated crossroads.

But, first, back to my new assignment as Assistant to the Director of Footwear Marketing and Manufacturing with my focus to be on the marketing side.

As you have already seen, Nelson Carmichael was a very capable executive. He immediately began to involve me in all aspects of his marketing responsibility. Charm Step continued to report directly to me. As I began to understand the overall structure he gradually transferred other divisions to my oversight. By 1969 all domestic Footwear Marketing reported to me and I was made a Corporate Vice President.

Managing the marketing functions was very different from manufacturing and I had a lot to learn. I was very fortunate to have a highly experienced and capable group of division heads who quickly got me oriented. Obviously some were a little frustrated with the idea of reporting to a guy whose main experience was in the manufacturing side of the business. But, before long, we were working together smoothly. And, frankly, I loved the new challenge! And we grew and prospered.

As usual Nelson was a great, hardworking boss. We got along well. And then one day he was gone. At a meeting at his church he had a heart attack and died. What a shock and loss to his family, friends, Genesco and especially to me.

In my judgment Eli White would have been the best Genesco Executive to succeed Nelson but he had left the company some time before to become President and CEO of a large competitor. As a result I was selected to succeed Nelson and in 1972 became Vice President and Group President of Genesco Footwear Marketing and Manufacturing not including International. This also caused me to fill Nelson's former seat on the corporate Executive Committee. This all could be described as a major career crossroad. But it might be better called an introduction to the Devil's Roller Coaster!

## My Dad

Before letting you experience the roller coaster I want to tell you of some important non - business developments. My dad had developed diabetes in 1956 and it gradually worsened. By the early sixties his vitality and mobility were severely impaired but his mind was clear. After a setback (Leukemia for several years complicated by a recent pneumonia attack) it was necessary for him to be in the hospital. After leaving work on January 18, 1965 I stopped by to visit with him. He was in good spirits and we had a spirited discussion. About 10 P.M. he said "Son, you have been at work all day and must be worn out. Quint is coming up from Florence, Alabama and will be here soon. Go home and I'll see you tomorrow." Quint (my doctor brother) arrived about 11:30 P.M. and found that after I left Dad had tried to get out of bed, fell and had a serious reaction. He called me at once and I got back to the hospital about midnight. Quint had called Brother Witt (Kingsport – 5 hours away) and Mom. From his exam and conference with Dad's doctor Quint felt that this was likely to be terminal. Dad never regained consciousness and died about 6 A.M. on January 19 with Mom, Quint, Witt and me at his bedside. It's hard to explain how sad we were. For years I could not get over "what might have been" if I had waited for Quint to arrive. I have missed him more than I can explain.

## 6001 Andover Drive.

In 1959 Mickey and I decided to move to a larger home and bought a house on Melbourne Dr. near the Sequoia Club, a fine swimming and tennis club, and Percy Priest Elementary School. We liked the area and a few years later bought a beautiful lot nearby where we hoped to build our "Dream Home". Kathy had found the lot which was on a dead end street – Andover Dr. and next door to one of her girlfriends. They played on the lot which had a magnificent sycamore tree which many years later won the "Biggest Tree" award for the county. As we began to create the plans for the new home I often asked Dad who had spent a lifetime in the building business for advice. He made important suggestions which we used but which he never saw because he died before the home was finished. Kathy learned to drive by each day driving me to inspect the building progress.

We moved to our new home 6001 Andover Drive in 1966 and ,except for five years in Philadelphia which you will read about later, this has been our home place ever since.

## The Devil's Roller Coaster

In order to understand my "Devil's Roller Coaster" it's important to be aware of transitions taking place in Genesco and in its Senior Management. From the rapidly growing footwear company that I had joined in 1948, we had gone through a major expansion of this base and rapid expansion through acquisition of apparel companies, non-related retailers (Bonwit Teller, Tiffany etc.), European companies, etc. There was great concern about this expansion which led to internal management battles. Frank Jarman, Maxey's son, replaced his father as CEO. A number of other upper level management changes occurred.

## Frank Jarman

When I joined the Executive Committee the membership consisted of Chairman (Frank Jarman), Two Vice Chairs (Larry Shelton and Ralph Bowles), Two Group Presidents (Ed Carney and me). Frank was a very bright but also a very opinionated executive who relied on input from sometimes flawed sources in the company. My first exposure to this came shortly after I had succeeded Nelson as Group President – Footwear. Ralph Bowles the Vice Chairman to whom I now reported, asked me to come by his office. His message was "You need to fire Felix Weiseger". (Felix headed all Footwear Retail operations and was the best and most experienced retailer in our organization.) Of course, I was shocked and asked – why? His answer was "Frank doesn't want him in "His" company." After vigorous discussion it became clear that Felix was out - whether I told him or someone else did – He was out!

I went to see Felix. When I entered his office he smiled and said "Good Morning, George, I've been expecting you. Frank wants me out, doesn't he?" And then he explained that in the corporate battle between Maxey and son Frank for control of the company Felix had supported Maxey! Welcome to Corporate Politics!

My relationship with Frank was touch and go. On the positive side he invited me to be a member of the Tyler Cup Team. This was a four man team that traveled to Dallas yearly to have exhaustive physical exams and to compete in the Tyler Cup Races against other corporate teams. The four of us traveled together on the company plane and got along quite well.

On the negative side, he was a second guesser and was determined to inject himself into the decision making within the operating groups. He also made arbitrary decisions about managers within the groups. On one occasion Ralph came by my office, sat down and said "Frank wants you to fire Lee Binkley." I almost fell out of my seat! Lee was the Human Resources (Industrial Relations) Director for the Footwear group. He had been with General Shoe / Genesco for many years. He was highly respected by our whole organization. I was shocked, angry and ready to fight! I wanted to confront Frank! Ralph said "Wait, George. Larry (the other vice chair whose responsibility included corporate human resources) and I have been arguing this issue for a month with Frank and he won't budge. If you confront him we may lose you also and we don't want that to happen. Please talk to Larry first."

So I did. We had a long discussion which led to a plan. He and Ralph were never able to explain why Frank had it in for Lee. The plan was: Lee was then 55 and would lose 10 years of retirement accumulation plus no Genesco income for 10 years until normal retirement. Steps would be taken to permit Lee to retire at 55 with retirement income equal to what he would have received at age 65 if his salary stayed the same for the ten years. It helped but I never forgave Frank for this arbitrary humiliation of a longtime, loyal employee. It did greatly increase my respect for Larry Shelton, another Paducahn – Well, close! He comes from Lone Oak just outside Paducah city limits! ☺

## And Then There was the Hardy Store Episode

In 1977 I was now Executive Vice President and General Manager of all domestic and international footwear activities. We had 46 factories, 1200 retail stores, over 300 wholesale salesmen, 3 tanneries, and many warehouses, shipping rooms, etc. in the United States and Canada. We had established offices in Spain, Italy, Brazil, South Korea and Hong Kong to create additional sources of supply for our wholesale and retail operations.

In the U.S. we were constantly opening new retail stores as new malls opened or we expanded into new regions. Of course, new stores required capital investments and Frank required that the cost to open each new store must be approved by the Executive Committee. He was very critical of the retail architects we used and finally demanded that we do a ground up analysis of a new Hardy Store in San Antonio, Texas with competitive bids on each component. After a month or so of intensive work by the Hardy organization I brought their request to the Executive Committee. After a full morning debating the proposal the vote was 4-1 in favor with only Frank opposing. I will never forget his reaction. He said "Well, ____ ____ I will agree provided you remove the water fountain and the hot water heater and disconnect the heat side of the air conditioning and heating system. Heat from the overheard lights should be enough."

About 2:00 A.M. the next morning our phone rang. It was Ralph and he said "What are you doing?" and I said "Trying to sleep!" and then he told me that he and Larry were at his place talking (Only a few blocks away) and wanted me to join them. I did. We talked the rest of the night about what needed to be done about the "Frank Jarman" problem.

All of this ultimately led to a decision by the Board to remove Frank from the Board and from his executive position at Genesco. A Search Committee was created to find a new C.E.O. Ralph, Larry and I were ruled out of consideration since we were the "revolutionists" who started the revolution.

See what I mean about the "Devil's Roller Coaster"! It gets worse!

## The Search – Jack Hanigan

The Board engaged Jack Hanigan, a retired Brunswick Industry executive, to do the search. After some time with no result, the Board decided to forget the search and employ Hanigan as the new C.E.O. Jack immediately set about installing some new ground rules for the Senior Executives. One of these I detested and it immediately got me in hot water with Jack.

He felt that senior officers should not eat in the cafeteria but should have a private dining room with waiters, etc. The cafeteria was important to me since it provided an opportunity for me to interact with "The Troops" and get input from a broad assortment of our employees. He did not like my continued visits to the cafeteria.

He was a strong believer in the benefits to be gained by Senior Executives from the A.M. P. Program at Harvard (Advanced Management Program). The program provided 13 weeks of case study supported training to rising senior executives from all over the world. It is an impressive program and gave the opportunity to learn and to compare yourself to top executives from all over. Larry was our first executive to attend and I went next in 1978

He also was convinced that countries like China were the manufacturing wave of the future and urged me to accelerate our work there. We already had an import office in Hong Kong and South Korea but no presence in China. As a result, I visited Japan and China in 1979 with one of our marketing directors, Fowler Low and the manager of our Hong Kong Office. We arranged for key Chinese officials to visit with us in Nashville so we could begin an import relationship.

During 1980 our footwear organization continued to perform well but Jack was constantly coming up with new ideas for us to try. And then in late 1980 he came to my office, sat down and said – "I want you to close all of the domestic shoe factories! Now!" (There were 46) I said "Jack, you must be kidding!" His reply "No___ ____ I want it done!" and I said "Jack, our whole branded sales organization and our 1200 retail stores depend on the plants for their products. We are moving rapidly to strengthen our foreign sourcing but we're far from ready. This would be a financial disaster". Again he said "I want it done now!"

And I replied "Ok, Mr. Hanigan, If you will put this in a written order to me I will do it." He got red as a beet and stormed out of my office. We didn't speak for the next 2 months and I got no written order.

And then at a management meeting he announced a new program which I strongly opposed. After the meeting I went to his office and told him of my opposition and that since we didn't see things the same way I would take early retirement (I was 55) and get out of his way. He thought that was a good idea. My days at Genesco after 35 years were over!

The "Devil's Roller Coaster" was now over too. That night Mickey and I went to a favorite Chinese restaurant and when I opened my fortune cookie it said "Do not fear change- It's all for the better!" I still have the fortune and it was right!

# Chapter 11

# Family, Farm, Langstaff Landing

- The Family

- Tennessee Angles Farm

- Langstaff Landing

## The Family

"The Seventies" was a decade of colleges and marriages for our family. As the year 1969 ended, Trish who was then 21, married her college boyfriend Charles Poole. They settled down at Birmingham-Southern College (in Birmingham, Alabama) while Charles finished his last semester there. After Charles finished college and without my knowledge he applied for a job at Genesco in our chemical division (one of my responsibilities). What a surprise when I saw his name on a list of new supervisors.

In February 1973 Lynne (22) married Steve Frederick a Birmingham – Southern College classmate. She graduated in May of 1973 and later received her Master's Degree from the University of Alabama-Birmingham. Steve received his Doctorate in Dental Medicine and they settled in Gadsden, Alabama

In 1975 Kathy (22) graduated from Peabody College (now a part of Vanderbilt). In 1976 she married Greg Haag and a few years later (while Mickey and I lived in Philadelphia) they lived in our home on Andover Drive and grandson Greg, Jr. was born while they lived there.

And now Mickey and I were alone on Andover Drive. I consider the successful raising of our wonderful daughters to be the greatest accomplishment of our life together. That process was FULL of crossroads successfully navigated! I would need to live to be 100 in order to describe them all.

## Tennessee Angles Farm

During the Christmas holiday of 1975, Kathy and Greg were visiting with us and we got to talking about farms. (I can't remember how the subject came up.) Greg's Dad, Bud, was a well-respected realtor and at one point Greg said that his Dad was also on vacation like I was so maybe we could look at some farms. And the next day Bud and I went to look at several farms that were on the market.

My Dad had often told me his concept for selecting and buying a farm:

1. Select a city which had strong prospects for growth

2. Determine which counties surrounding the city were showing the best management and growth possibilities

3. Having identified the target county determine the least developed segment of the county

4. Drive into that segment until you reach the beginning of rural mail delivery

5. Go 15-20 miles further and start looking for your farm

Bud thought I was nuts but he agreed with my conclusion on 1, 2, 3(Nashville-Williamson County-West toward Centerville). So that night he put together a list of farms for sale in our target zone. And we went looking. I also hoped to get a farm that had a creek and a lake.

After looking at 5 or 6 farms only one appealed to me and we cut across a different road to go back and look at it again. We had gone a short distance when we saw a sign saying "Farm for Sale by Owner." So, what the heck! Let's go see it!

When we got there the gate was locked but we could see an attractive cottage and barn across a little creek in a nice valley. I looked at Bud, he looked at me, and we climbed the fence and walked down to the cottage and then to the barn. Once at the barn I could see a small pond so I walked to see it. As I turned from the pond to go back to the barn I caught a reflection from water some distance beyond the pond. It was 1 ½ acre lake. Wow!

When we got back home Bud set about contacting the owner to get a full plat of the farm, the price, etc., etc.  The next day son-in-law Steve Frederick (Lynne's husband) and I walked the full boundary of the farm, inspected the house, barn, lake etc.  Much to my joy it all looked like my dream farm.

That afternoon Bud came over and we discussed what to do. The farm acreage was 144 and the asking price was $75,000. ($529/acre). I had received a nice $20,000 bonus just before Christmas so I proposed to offer: "$70,000; $20,000 down; $10,000 for five years paid on January 1 + 5% interest on the balance.

Bud left and we waited and waited. Finally, he got back with a frown on his face. We sat down in a circle: Bud, Steve, Lynne, Mickey and me. With the frown on his face he looked at me, burst into a smile and said "Congratulations! You're a farmer!" Now, <u>Talk about a crossroad- this was a big one!</u>

It ultimately played an enormous role in our lives. You will see some things about the farm in this narrative but at this time I will simply say that <u>this purchase was one of the very best decisions of our life.</u>

We named the farm "Tennessee Angles" after "The Angles", home of Great Grandfather Quintus Quincy Quigley in Paducah, Ky. (more on QQQ later) (and much more on the "Tennessee Angles".)

## Langstaff Landing

Back in the late 1940's and early 1950's my Mom and Dad visited several times in Destin, Florida with Russell and Mary Martin, the partners in the construction of " The Cabin" back in Paducah days, who had a new cottage in a place named Four Mile Village, Destin Florida. This 500+ acre "Village" with a quarter mile of beach frontage had been a military base during World War II where captured German V-2 rockets and our version of them were test fired out over the Gulf of Mexico. After the war, the Coffeen Family retrieved their property and began a very deliberate approach to turning it into a nature-oriented private community. After several visits Mom and Dad were approved by the Coffeens as prospective property owners and they started to look. At that time lots on the beach sold for about $10,000 and on the 55 acre lake they were $5,000. Dad was fly fishing in his canoe (carried on the car from Nashville) on the lake and as he approached a lot he had looked at, he made a cast and – BAM! A big strike! And he landed an 8 ½ lb bass! Voila! He bought the lot!

His intent was to design a cottage beside the lake and he worked on plans for several years but in 1956 he came down with Leukemia and his energy level dropped dramatically. He never got it built before he died in 1965.

Mom continued to stay in their home after Dad's death and worked at the Vanderbilt Library. On at least one night a week she would have dinner with us. Around 1970 she started saying that she needed to be home by 8:30. We were puzzled until she confessed that her high school boyfriend, Johnny Pierson, now a widower, was calling her at 8:30 every night. We had heard a lot about "Johnny" over the years and were glad when she told us that he was coming for a visit. I asked Mom if she wanted me to go to the airport with her. She declined the offer and went by herself. This was in the days when greeters waited behind a fence as the plane taxied in and discharged the passengers. Johnny got off of the plane walked through the gate and right past Mom.

Later when I told him that Mom told me he had walked right past her he said "Heck, I was looking for an 18 year old girl!" Soon they were married and had 17 wonderful years before his death.

Johnny was a successful banker in Gainesville, Florida and over the years was very helpful to Mom in managing her estate. When it was apparent that nothing was being done with the lot in Four Mile Village, Florida he urged her to give the lot to her three sons. Mom thought that was a good idea. She contacted Dorothy Coffeen, the owner- manager of the village to get it done. Dorothy would not permit multiple ownership so the idea stalled. Then Mickey and I talked to brothers Witt and Quint about the idea of having the lot appraised and we would buy their share. They liked it. The appraisal was $15,000 triple Dad's purchase price. We did the deal. And then we began to think about what to do with the lot. By 1977 we had a serious plan in hand and engaged Fort Walton Beach (near Destin) architect Warren Lisenbee to review it. He made excellent changes and we were ready to go.

Mickey and I made a special trip to Destin to meet with Dorothy Coffeen and review our plans to make sure they met the building guidelines for Four Mile Village. She made a couple of minor changes which we accepted.

We had met a retired military officer, Jack Ryan, who was building houses in the area and asked him to give us a bid. He did. It seemed reasonable ($55,000) and we said go. Working with his son-in–law Jim Riehle, a retired Marine flyer, they did a great job and completed the house in 1978. We, our children, grandchildren, great grandchildren, and friends have enjoyed this wonderful, quiet spot on the Gulf for over 34 years. It has been a truly, positive crossroad in many lives. P.S. Jim Riehle to this day continues to maintain Langstaff Landing and keeps it in top shape.

# Chapter 12

# A Call From the Footwear Industry

- So what happened after "The Devil's Roller Coaster?"

- The American Shoe Center

- Focus of My Business Activity For 4 ½ Years

- The Team

## So, what happened after the "Devil's Roller Coaster?"

A week or so after my last confrontation with Hanigan, I started considering what I would like to do now. A top consideration was rural real estate. And then came a call from Peter Solomon owner of a shoe company in Boston. He and Dick Shomaker, President of Brown Shoe in St. Louis, wanted to come to see me. They had heard about my "early retirement" and wanted me to consider an idea they had. I knew them both well since we served on the A.F.I.A. (American Footwear Industry Association) Board together and played tennis at every annual gathering. We had a good visit. Their idea was that the new footwear industry Advanced Technology Center in Philadelphia was in dire need of strong, industry-knowledgeable leadership and I was just right for the job. I agreed to meet them in Philly and take a look.

I was impressed with the efforts being made to identify the best shoemaking systems and technologies and assist the domestic industry in learning and using them. So, what the heck, let's consider it. The salary would be the same as Genesco including a stipend for our home cost in Philly. Mickey liked the idea so I started looking for a place to live. One of the center supervisors, hearing about my farm, told me about a farm in nearby Wayne, PA. that occasionally had homes for rent. He gave me a phone number for Alex Wheeler who worked at the University of Pennsylvania Medical Center just a couple of blocks from the Footwear Center. We talked for quite a while and then he said "Why don't you come out for supper tonight and I can show you the property." The cottage he was going to show me was vacant because he had recently gotten married and moved to his new wife's home. I urged him to check with her first if he wanted the marriage to last. He did. It was OK and I went to dinner. Before dinner we went to see "The Cottage". Holy Mackerel ! "The cottage" was a 21 room mansion, fully furnished and set in the middle of a 250 acre dairy cattle farm (Ardrossen). Man! Was I impressed! But my heart sank because I knew it would be far too expensive.

After supper (which was great) we sat around and talked. They must have asked me a hundred questions about myself, my family, my new position etc. and then he said that they wanted us in the house and the rent would be--- and he stated the exact amount that was in my contract with the Shoe Center!! We agreed with a handshake and lived in that magnificent home for our five years in Philadelphia. We visited Alex and Grace at their home on the Maine Coast and they visited us at our Four Mile Village cottage in Florida. We became very good friends and stayed in touch until he died years later. I never found out whether or not someone at The Shoe Center had given him my contract arrangement.

## The American Shoe Center/F.I.A.

It didn't take us long to move what few items of furniture, etc. we needed into the beautifully equipped house on Church St in Wayne, PA called Ardrossen. Newlyweds Kathy and Greg Haag, Sr. moved into 6001 Andover and lived there while we were "Up East". We settled in and I started my daily commute to The Shoe Center in Downtown Philly. I had a Volkswagen and drove most days. 52 stoplights from home to office! It took me a while to get familiar with the timing of the lights but ultimately got down to about 8-10 stops.

The center was intended to be a testing laboratory available to the industry at large and a training center to provide classes in state of the art manufacturing technology and systems. It was closely allied with Satra, an English footwear technology research organization, which was noted worldwide for the excellence of its work.

Of course, my first objective was to get acquainted with the staff and develop an understanding of their skills and exactly what they provided to the industry. Also, of great importance was evaluation of the membership base to determine how broadly the total U.S. footwear industry was represented. It was apparent that in both areas there was work to be done. However, a good job had been done to assemble a competent base of technology skills and of experienced shoemakers to create believable educational courses. There were some weaknesses which were soon overcome.

Within six months it became increasingly obvious to the Boards of the Shoe Center and the American Footwear Industries Association (AFIA) in Washington DC that there was great overlapping of activities. Maybe we should consider merging the two organizations. Many of the members served on both Boards. We decided to have a joint board meeting to discuss the issue. It concluded that a merger should take place. I was asked to handle the merger with our law firms and become the C.E.O. of the new organization – Footwear Industries of America (F.I.A.).

This change made a huge difference in my situation since now I also became deeply involved in industry political and lobbying activities as well as our major industry shoe shows.

I now started to spend 2-3 days a week in Washington. Again Mickey was a good sport and took all of this in stride. She became a volunteer guide at the historic Paoli, PA home of Gen. Anthony Wayne. Also, since I was now a member of Satra's Council (Board) we traveled to England twice a year for their meetings. Often we would schedule a week of vacation at meeting time, rent a car and search for our family roots in

England and Scotland. We found the very cottage in the North Riding of Yorkshire that my Langstaff ancestors built in 1630.

In Wayne we soon developed a fine group of friends and tennis players who helped to keep us occupied. Most exciting to us was the fact that nearby in New Jersey was Mount Holly which was where around 1680 my ancestors settled after leaving England for the U.S.A. We found good friends and distant cousins in the Stacy Moore Family. On many visits back and forth they helped us come to know and love our early roots.

Another great benefit of life in Philadelphia was the opportunity to see that part of our country in a much more detailed way. If I timed it right I could leave my office and be in Grand Central Station, New York in 1 ½ hours or in Washington in 2 ½ hours. And all this by Amtrak!

## Focus of My Business Activity for 4 ½ Years

Now, let me write a little about the state of the U.S. footwear industry and the role of F.I.A. in addressing key challenging issues. Since the end of World War II, the U.S. manufacturing industries including footwear and apparel had experienced dramatic growth as shortages were filled in war ravaged areas which were still without competitive industrial bases. The U.S.A., under wartime rationing also had created shortages in almost all civilian goods. But by the 1970's things were changing - Europe was showing much progress, the emerging countries like Japan, China, Korea, India, Brazil, Mexico, Etc., were focusing on labor intensive industries such as footwear and apparel and it was beginning to hurt. The wage rate comparisons were a real challenge. Government regulations in the U.S.A. were far more restrictive than in these countries. U.S. retailers, as economic theories predict, were looking for the lowest prices and this was really beginning to pinch American footwear and apparel manufacturers. American productivity in products per man hour continued to be far superior to foreign competitors but our mandatory minimum wage laws created a more than 10-1 cost of labor per hour disadvantage with the emerging countries, Our edge in products per man hour could not come close to overcoming this difference.

So- what can the footwear industry trade association (F.I.A.) do to help overcome this challenge?

Let's look first at what our human resources were to attack the problem.

## The Team

Legal- Tom Shannon, Lauren Howard

Congressional Contacts – Fawn Evenson

Financial Skills – Diane Dineen

Membership Relations – Daniyel Steinberg

Manufacturing Expertise – Lee McKinley

Presenters –

- George Langstaff & Fawn Evenson from F.I.A.

- Top Execs from Member Companies and Unions

And then the big question –

(1) What should our strategy be?

(2) How should we implement it?

(3) When?

With the F.I.A. Board approval the team set about answering the questions. Very simply stated the answers were:

(1) Under the International Trade Laws tariff relief was acceptable when unfair competition could be proven.

Therefore, we should build a legal case to prove unfair competition and create a groundswell of support within the industry and especially from states in which our industry was an important employer.

(2) Fawn Evenson, our Director of Government Relations, working with our legal counsel should create the legal case for presentation to Congress; layout the plan for rallies, lobbying, fundraising, public relations activities etc.; and assume general oversight of the effort.

(3) The questions of when to file would be dependent on how soon the case could be drawn up and industry support could be generated. But work would start on all of this right away.

I could write many pages on the terrific job done by this team; the hundreds of visits with members of Congress; the many rallies of footwear workers and union members; the MANY speeches and appearances made on talk shows by me and key industry executives and even a style show in Washington featuring Senator Al Gore and wife.

Congress voted in favor of our case and sent it to President Reagan for his approval. He vetoed it under extreme pressure from the retail industry. We went back to Congress for an override and failed by one vote.

A year or so later we went through it all again. Won in Congress. Vetoed. Override failed again by one vote. I was sick at heart. I had tried my very best to save an industry that I dearly loved and failed. This was in 1985.

After much thought and since I had agreed to take the association job for three years and I had now been there five years I told the Board that I had done all that I knew to do and failed, so I would give 6 months' notice  and let someone else try.

The whole industry was very gracious and threw a fantastic retirement party at "Tavern on the Green" in New York with several hundred of my industry friends in attendance. Our daughters and sons-in-law plus two grandchildren (Sam and Krista) were there. Mom flew in from Florida forgetting it was cold in New York! We kept her warm! ☺ Witt and Helen came also from Tennessee. Our family was well represented. The industry gave us a terrific "Going Away" gift – a fully paid trip for two to the next Wimbledon Tennis Tournament. What a great gift for two old tennis players!! And we had a ball!

And thus ended my thirty eight years in the footwear industry. I did consult for fifteen years after that. So, all told, 53 years in footwear.

Epilogue: Try to find a new pair of shoes now that is made in the U.S.A.! Almost impossible to do! What a shame!

# Chapter 13

# <u>A New Life Begins</u>

- Do What You Want To Do

- The Farm

- Four Mile Village (Langstaff Landing)

- Topsail Hill

- St. George's Episcopal Church

- Special Trips

## A New Life Begins

### It's Called – Do What You Want To Do!

As we left our wonderful home and friends in Philadelphia and settled back into life in Nashville it was like opening Pandora's Box! What did we want to do – OK- Do it!

Our list was long and we had a lot of fun sorting through how we would best utilize our new free time. Highlights to consider included:

- Serious farming on Tennessee Angles Farm

- Long periods at Langstaff Landing

- Resume active role at Four Mile Village

- Plan and execute our long wanted overseas travel plan

  - Australia, New Zealand

  - Northern Europe- Denmark, Norway, Sweden, Finland, Russia, Poland, Germany, Holland, London

  - Western Europe – Belgium, France, Italy, Switzerland, Germany

  - England, Scotland, Ireland

  - Normandy

  - Japan and China

  - Delta Queen on Mississippi River

  - Middle East

  - Alaska

  - Hawaii

- More time with our expanding family

## The Farm

Immediately I began to spend time at the farm. There was much to do. Fences were in bad shape and I started on them as a one man fence builder. Lloyd Green who managed the cattle and had worked with me from the time of purchase would help when two men were required. Lloyd is the one who gave me one of my early farming lessons.

One September day in the late 1970's it was time to round up the cattle, give them shots, castrate the bull calves, de-horn as required, etc. I was new and didn't know how to do anything but wanted to help. Once we got the cattle inside the corral it was necessary to separate a cow and run it down a chute into the head catcher where it would be held in place while the doctoring went on. Well, I felt that I could do that so, that was my job.

After I got several in the chute and caught, I was sorta proud of myself until, on the next one, I ran into the electric fence and got shocked on the neck. A little later I did it again and this time on one ear. Finally, I hit it a third time on my forehead. Lloyd threw his knife down and said "Heck, Mr. Langstaff, my mule is smarter than that!" They never let me forget that one.

And from there I learned to do it all. Caring for the cattle; cutting, raking and baling hay; bush hogging; fertilizing the fields etc. And I loved it!

Ultimately I found that mid-April to June 1 and October 1 to November 15 would be good periods to be in Destin since farm work load dropped way off. And more or less from then until now we have planned 6 weeks in the Spring and 6 weeks in the Fall for our time at Langstaff Landing.

## Four Mile Village (Langstaff Landing)

Shortly after returning to Nashville and on one of our six weeks visits I was elected to the Village Board and soon appointed as chair of the "Save the Hammock Committee". A "hammock" is a segment of land in a tropical forest in which deciduous trees exist in small patches. Within the 500 acres of Four Mile Village there is a large tropical forest with about a 3-4 acre hammock. Our hammock is adjacent to the magnificent 1800 acre tract of ancient forest being threatened by aggressive development plans.

Our initial committee discussions centered on the observation that, what good would it do to "save" the 4 acre hammock if our neighboring 1800 acres turned into a high rise development!?

## Topsail Hill

So, with my new video camera, I produced a 10 minute video of the highlights of the 1800 acre Topsail Hill tract and sent it to The Nature Conservancy for their comments and recommendations. Almost immediately I had a call from George Willson of the Conservancy offering to come meet with us and help us map a strategy. Wow! From a 5 person committee we now had the Conservancy swelling our ranks.

To make a long, complex process shorter I will summarize the result. We ultimately organized "Citizens for the Preservations of Topsail Hill" – 1300 citizens. We lobbied local officials and the Governor and his cabinet in Tallahassee. (I got help from my old Washington law firm on some of this). Our lawyers found improper financial transactions on parcels within the tract. Property values were improperly overstated on many Savings and Loan notes which helped lead to the Savings and Loans crisis. As a result, the 1800 acres was to be auctioned along with other properties in Walton County.

On the day of the auction Mickey and I were in Tallahassee early for me to speak to the Governor and his Cabinet again and urge their authorization for the Conservancy to bid in the auction on behalf of the State of Florida. Several others spoke before my time came. When my name was called Governor Childs said "Mr. Langstaff, we have heard you several times. It's my feeling that the cabinet is ready to vote but if you want to speak the floor is yours. And I said "Thank you, Governor. I think I will sit down. "I did. They did. The vote was favorable. I immediately called George Willson who was at the court house in DeFuniak Springs, Florida awaiting the result of the Cabinet vote. He was now authorized to bid on behalf of the State of Florida!

Mickey and I piled into the car and drove as fast as we could to DeFuniak. As I skidded into the Courthouse parking lot we could see our several hundred members cheering and throwing hats in the air. The bidding was over! Topsail Hill would now be a Florida Preserve!! And, also, the Conservancy successfully bid on an additional 18,000 acres of non- coastal Walton County property which over the years has been used for county offices, schools, police and fire locations, etc. Thanks for hammocks!! What a gift this was to Florida, Walton County and all of us! As Chairman of the Citizens Group I consider this one of the best crossroads I have experienced.

This was only the beginning of the many challenges and joys of being a part of Four Mile Village. The 40+ property owners represented a broad geographical swath from California to North Carolina and Iowa to Texas. Backgrounds are very varied- Doctors, Lawyers, French Navy Seaman in World War I, Business Executives, Teachers, Pro Football Team owner, realtors, bankers, retired military, preacher, fire chief etc. All successful and, therefore, bright but also opinionated, Most of them you liked a lot but a few you wanted to knock on the head! ☺ But we found ways to work together and manage what I consider a beautiful peaceful and, actually, unique village.

We have been blessed with two sets of wonderful caretakers - George and Lucille Bishop and, after their retirement, Bruce and Susan Paladini. It has been my honor to serve four terms on the Board and three terms as President. Daughter, Lynne, now serves on the Board as Secretary (2012).

Our cottage gets lots of use by family and friends. (No rentals) We have a family rule for use of the cottage. "If you are a family member (beyond college) you may let any of your friends use the cottage— provided that you are with them!" Daughter Trish is in charge of scheduling. A modest fee/day is paid to Mickey to cover utility cost. And you better follow the close up instructions or else! ☺

## St. George's Episcopal Church

Once back in Nashville we took up where we left off at St. George's Episcopal Church. At the time we left I was on the Vestry and my good friend, Charlie Brown, who was now the Senior Warden insisted that I run for the Vestry again. Since I had twisted his arm some years back to get him to run I just couldn't say "No". I was elected and served through some tough times which included an unpleasant change of Clergy Leadership.

Also, while we were away a new and very impressive sanctuary had been built. Time has proven the wisdom of this action. But, early on, it brought some financial challenges which had to be addressed. Today (2012) it is a vibrant, growing church with some 3500 members and a top flight clergy staff headed by the Rev Leigh Spruill, a real leader!

Over the years I have been honored to serve 15 years on the Vestry and 3 terms as Senior Warden. This has been a Christian crossroad which I cherish.

## Special Trips

Over the years a number of important and interesting trips have been made. Some by me alone but mostly by Mickey and me together. Collectively, this wide travel has provided a better understanding of the world we live in and the amazing diversity of people. I'm listing these with terse comments to give you an idea of why I say that:

1970 – Italy, Yugoslavia, Germany, France, England by Mickey and me to visit key European footwear companies and "Broaden my perspective of what it's like in the sophisticated fashion world." Trip initiated by Genesco's President to help me transition from a shoemaker to a marketing executive.

1978 - Brazil, Spain, Italy, Switzerland, Germany and England. Visits by me to get acquainted with our South American and European offices and contacts after Genesco's international functions were included in my responsibilities.

1978 - Japan, China, South Korea, Hong Kong by Mickey and me and our International Director Fowler Low. Same objective as above.

1980 -1985 –England- During this five years Mickey and I were in England many times for Satra Council meetings and often added vacation weeks in which we explored England and Scotland from top to bottom. Self-driving, wrong side of the road!

1984 - Germany, Switzerland, France by Mickey and me with good friends Ernie and Dot Moench. We attended Pirmasen's, a very important International Footwear Show, in Germany and then went sightseeing. Self-Driving.

1987 - Australia, New Zealand, Hawaii by Mickey and me with Dot and Ernie Moench. One of the best trips we ever made. We fell in love with New Zealand. If the U.S.A. goes down the drain then look for us in New Zealand or Switzerland.

1989 – Scandinavia, Russia, Poland, Germany (just before the wall went down) Holland, England with Witt and Helen. Probably the most eye opening and educational trip of all.

1995 – Alaska with just the two of us. If you haven't done this one, then do it! Part of the trip was on "The Spirit of Alaska" a wonderful small ship carrying 85 passengers. Magnificent scenery! Alaska made 49 states visited for Old George. Still missing North Dakota

1996 – Ireland- Mickey and me. No business. Just fun as we drove all around that beautiful place. The Irish people are really special. If you go, don't miss their pubs! Found many traces of early Quigley family. Stayed first night at B& B run by a Quigley Family .(much more on the Quigleys later)

1996 – Cancun, Mexico- with our entire immediate family to celebrate our 50<sup>th</sup> Wedding Anniversary. Had a great time seeing the sights, enjoying the beach, etc. One day I walked about a mile down the beach to visit with Wayne and Laura Dugas, friends from Four Mile Village and their family. More about these folks when I tell you about "The Sponsors"

1998 – <u>China</u> - Mickey and I took a Yangtze River Cruise and Tour. Since our first visit 20 years earlier the changes were mind blowing! The tour covered Beijing, Shanghai, and the Yangtze up to Chongqing then to Xian and down to Hong Kong. Very interesting to see the enormous progress being made. In Shanghai Airport during a storm delay a lovely young Chinese girl Zhou Qian Qian came over to Mickey and asked if she could practice her English. We ultimately met her whole family since we were flying to Wuhan their home. We stayed in touch with Qian Qian by email and regular mail since then. She is now happily married. If you ever have a chance to make this trip do it. You won't regret it.

1999 - <u>West Yellowstone, ID</u>- Art and Char Hancock invited us to spend a week at their cottage here and what a great time we had. We covered Yellowstone Park from top to bottom, were guests on a friends boat on the lake, on the way back we all visited with Cousin Dody and Benny Hoff in Ketchum, ID. Art, who was the Jack Daniels' Marketing Director when it's terrific marketing strategy was developed, brought them a fifth of Jack Daniels whiskey which was well received! ☺

2000 - <u>Steamboat Delta Queen</u> – From St. Louis, MO to St. Paul, MN with Scottie and Jim Haynes a Harvard "Can" mate. Having grown up on the Tennessee and Ohio Rivers and them worked on a Mississippi River Tug Boat that regularly visited St. Louis this was a joyful trip for me. And even though Mickey doesn't prefer boats she handled this well. And all were impressed with her ability to play the calliope. It was a great trip with spectacular scenery, interesting side trips, great entertainment and wonderful food. We would do this again! And did - see 2007.

2001 – <u>Normandy</u> - D-day and subsequent battles with good friends Art and Char Hancock. The Hancocks arranged the trip. Nashville friend Joe Thompson, who participated in Normandy activity as a reconnaissance pilot, got us in touch with Jeanine Gillingham of LeMolay-Litry who added enormously to our knowledge of the impact and results of the action from a French viewpoint. I walked the beaches, climbed into the German entrenchments and followed the action on my maps. At our farewell dinner Joe Thompson's friend, Jeanine, made a talk to our group about D-day and its impact, then a group member closed with a heart rending singing of "Danny Boy". We came away with deep respect for the men who fought and died here. Mickey's brother, Kenneth Black, was a member of Patton's, 3<sup>rd</sup> Army from the breakout at Normandy until Germany's surrender. A Paducah friend, Skip Skinner, died in the landing on a segment of the beach that I was able to walk across and view from the German entrenchments.

2007- <u>Another Delta Queen Trip</u> - from Memphis to New Orleans, this time with good friends Hap and Susan Castner. Our experience was as good as our first trip up North. Great shore excursion into Natchez, MS and its surrounding battle fields. As a long time Civil War buff this was a highlight for me. Another fine visit to Baton Rouge and nearby plantations. We stopped at Helena, Arkansas for a visit to town and a southern music performance. During my days working on the Mississippi Helena was the port where we filled up our barges with oil and then headed back up the river to Wood River just North of St. Louis. While the barges filled we spent time in Helena. It has changed very little.

2008- <u>My last canoe trip into the boundary waters of Canada and the U.S.</u> – I had talked so much to many friends about my canoe trips into the Quetico that a couple of them really got excited and wanted to go. The three of us were all in our late 70's and it was unlikely that we could handle the rigors of paddling in, setting up tent camping, etc. So I talked with Williams and Hall the outfitters I had used so often in the past. They had a fine suggestion. Instead of a week or more go for 3 days of fishing and stay in modern accommodations near International Falls, MN and Nester Falls, Canada. An outfitter "Tinker's Places" was set up to do these short trips. They made it easy for "Old Folks". Have a nice dinner. Sleep well in a modern cabin. Get up at six. Eat a fine breakfast. Gather your fishing gear and walk 50 yards to the dock. Climb into a sea plane by 7:00 A.M. fly to the lake of choice for that day, 25-30 minutes. Be met by a guide and canoes. Fish until noon. Have a guide - cooked lunch. Be back in the canoes by 1:30 P.M. fish until 5:30. Fly back. Have a great meal. Go to bed. Do it again the next day! Holy mackerel! That sounded too good to be true! But it was! We called it "The Old Geezers Special"! We caught lots of fish and had a great time. I will never see the Boundary Waters again but I can truly say that my trips there have been highlights in my life!

<u>The Old Geezers Were</u>

Bill Wadlington (Old Geezer)

Van Wadlington (Bill's Son)

Jeff Wadlington (Bill's Son)

Noel Sullivan (Old Geezer)

George Langstaff (Old Geezer)

Steve Frederick (George's Son-In- Law)

2010- <u>Mickey's North Carolina</u> – Mickey was born in North Carolina and over the years lived in many North Carolina towns. Her father was with Southern Bell Telephone and was often transferred to new locations as his career developed. In 2010 as I struggled for new gift ideas it struck me that a trip to her many homes there and to a meeting she had mentioned in Pinehurst might be well received. We did it and we traveled over 1500 miles. We attended the Pinehurst meeting first which focused on North Carolina. Then a long string of towns, houses, cousins, brothers, old schools etc. etc. etc. We also had a very interesting visit to the Billy Graham Museum and Library. We wound up in Kingsport, TN with a nice visit with my brother, Witt, and family. I won't say that this qualifies as a crossroad but I do think that I scored a few points! ☺

So why do I write about all of these trips in a book about the crossroads of my life? The best answer I can give is that without the trips and what they did to enhance my understanding of our world and its people I would have been a far less effective executive and far less motivated to undertake and resolve some of the challenges I faced. With certainty, I know that the trips with our daughters strengthened their understanding of this world we live in and their relationships with their parents and vice versa.

# Chapter 14

# <u>Happiness and Sadness</u>

- Family Developments

- Our Treasured Grandchildren

- Reunions

- John Black

- John Pierson

- Katherine Langstaff Pierson - Mom

- Mable Black

- Kenneth (Nick) Black

- John Black, Jr.

- Quintus Aden Langstaff

- Charles Poole

## Family Developments

Before going on to several important crossroads that have not yet been covered, I do want to cover important developments in family.

As any family history unfolds it reveals times of great joy and happiness. But it also reveals times of great sorrow and sadness. On the happiness side was the steady arrival of our fine grandchildren. This process was individually, and in total, one of the greatest and most welcome crossroads of my life. Each of our six grandchildren holds a special place in our hearts.

## Our Treasured Grandchildren

Sam Poole – 1972 – son of Trish and Charles. Early years in Nashville through Junior High then moved to Durham, NH through College. Now a banker in Williamsburg Va. with wife Tracy and two fine boys Jay and Reese.  During his teen years he was a devoted Boy Scout. While we lived in Philadelphia we visited his Boy Scout troop at the Annual Scout Jamboree in Virginia.

Jennifer Worley – 1977 – Daughter of George Stockman and Kathy Stockman's step daughter. Grew up with Kathy, George and Greg. She and Chris Worley have two impressive children – Daughter Taylor and Son Matthew. Jennifer holds an important job in Franklin, Tennessee and commutes from Murfreesboro.

Krista Carpenedo – 1978 – Daughter of Trish and Charles (see Sam above), our "Yankee", who spent her early years in Durham, NH. Fine athlete. Special interest in volleyball. Graduate of West Virginia Wesleyan University. Part time Coach and Recruiter at University of North Florida, Jacksonville, Florida. She and husband, Mike - a terrific golfer- Have two wonderful daughters Emmy and Kaia.

Scott Frederick – 1979 – Son of Lynne and Steve Frederick. Grew up in Gadsden Al. Graduate of Sewanee University and a graduate degree from Middlebury College. Two years in the Peace Corps (Kyrgyzstan.) Now in law school. Speaks Italian, Russian, Kyrgyz and Uzbek. Will be married in December 2012 to Alana Crowe, a classmate in law school. After completing his Peace Corps assignment he worked four years in Washington, DC with Chemonics International, a firm which manages U.S.A.I.D. programs all over the world. With his language skills his assignments were focused on Central and Southern Asia. He is now Editor in Chief of Law Review at Alabama School of Law and beginning to consider job possibilities after graduation

Todd Frederick – 1982 – Son of Lynne and Steve Frederick. Grew up in Gadsden, Al. graduate of Auburn University, University of Auburn Graduate degree and Cumberland School of Law at Samford University. He

106

and wife, Lindsay (Dr. of Obstetric Medicine) recently presented us with our youngest Great Grand Daughter, Caroline. They have now moved to Gadsden where Todd has set up his own Law Practice and Lindsay is joining a local obstetric practice. Lynne is the new and happy volunteer baby sitter.

Greg Haag, JR – 1983 – Son of Kathy and Greg Haag. We all regretted the failure of Kathy's first marriage but rejoice in the fact that it produced our fine grandson, Greg. For several years after her divorce she lived independently, took care of her son and worked to support them. It proved to Mickey and me that she was a truly tough and capable gal! Before long she married George Stockman who was divorced and had a young daughter, Jennifer. George became a fine "Father" for Greg and Kathy has been a fine "Mom" for Jennifer. Greg grew up largely in Murfreesboro, TN where he became a topflight baseball catcher. He then went to Montreat College in North Carolina. He had an outstanding baseball career and after graduation came back to Murfreesboro. He is now a successful Insurance rep for Liberty Mutual Insurance Company. (He saved us almost $2000 on our insurance) In August 2012 he married his beautiful college sweetheart – Carey Foster- Who has done all the typing for this book!

In summary, our grandchildren and great grandchildren are our greatest treasure. We are proud of them. Our success in life will be measured in the future by how well they conduct their lives. I have confidence.

## Reunions

Shortly after Mom married Johnny Pierson she started to worry about how her family would get to know Johnny's family. This resulted in a terrific series of Langstaff-Pierson Reunions which have been held every other year since 1973. We take turns being responsible for the planning and conduct of these fun events. They have been held in great locations all over the southeast. The last one was in 2011 in Destin, Florida. One of the nights was a buffet dinner at Langstaff Landing. We had over fifty attendees crowded into and onto the house and decks of Langstaff Landing. A great "Do you remember when?" event got the whole gang together to relish photos, videos, tall tales, etc. from our family past.

When Mom was still with us these events were highlights of her life. Johnny was a good sport and enjoyed them also but was snowed under by all those crazy Langstaffs. 2013 reunion near Gatlinburg, TN included 77 of our gang.

These were GREAT crossroads for Piersons and Langstaffs.

## Some of the Sad Moments

My life has included hundreds and hundreds of happy and inspiring experiences as have most lives. There have also been many events we would like to have avoided. But that's not to be. If I am to cover the crossroads of my life I need to describe negative ones as well as the positives.

1965 – George Q. Langstaff (Dad) (see page 77)

1978 - John Black (Mickey's Dad) (See Page 109)

1987 – <u>John Pierson</u> – Mom and Johnny had married in 1971 after Dad's death in 1965. They had a fine marriage and ultimately lived part of the year in Gainesville, FL (Johnny's home) and part in Newland, NC (up in the mountains). In mid-1980's Johnny was getting more and more feeble. Finally while they were in Newland they engaged a wonderful "mountain woman", Gloria Weinbarger, to live with them and care for him and for many housekeeping and driving issues. She became a "Family" member. In 1988 Johnny died after a long illness.

1992 – <u>Mom</u> – Shortly after Johnny's death her sons convinced Mom that she and Gloria should move to Nashville and live between there and Newland. This worked well and gave Mom an opportunity to get back in touch with old friends. They lived happily until 1992. At the normal time they left for their summer stay at Newland. Mom was in good health and her pacemaker had been checked out before she left Nashville.

They were having a great time in Newland where Mom had many friends. One day Mom and Gloria had gone to lunch with some friends. Had a great time. That night they watched favorite TV shows and then hit the sack.

The following morning when Gloria went to rouse Mom there was no response. Mom was lying peacefully in her bed but she was gone. Emergency came but there was no way they could help. Mom had died peacefully in her sleep.

This was one of the saddest days her family and friends ever experienced and yet, looking back, I have to say that she had been gently ushered into Heaven. How could there be a better way to leave this world? She was 89. Her sons would tell you that there could not have been a better mother!

1978- John Black – From the minute I first met John Black, Mickey's father, I liked him a lot and he liked me. I knew we would be friends whether I got to marry his daughter or not. Here was a man to admire. He started at the bottom climbing poles for Southern Bell Telephone and by the time I first met him was then in charge of all maintenance activity in South Carolina. He knew how to manage and inspire his teams. And what a great guy he was- Short; chubby but strong; great sense of humor; deeply intelligent; great fisherman; loved his granddaughters and they him; patient but yet demanding. Ok, to say it in a few worlds – He was my kind of guy!! A great father–in-law! And he loved to have tea parties with his grand daughters.

He was the source of one of my most important crossroads! His whole career until 1944 had been in North Carolina but in June of 1944 he was promoted to plant manager, South Carolina, and moved with his family to Columbia, S.C. His daughter, then at W.C. (Women's College of North Carolina) came along and enrolled at The University of South Carolina.

Now over in Atlanta about that time a young man got orders to go to a Navy unit at The University of South Carolina. And you know the rest of the story!

I called this "my most important crossroad" but, as I think about it, I believe the Lord was working in one of his mysterious ways!

While I was in the A.M.P. Program at Harvard in 1978 Dad Black was suffering from cancer and died after a lengthy illness. It was a major loss to our family!

1998 – Mable Black, Mickey's Mother, became a very good friend over the more than fifty years of our relationship. She and Dad Black met while she was a telephone switchboard operator with Southern Bell and he was a Southern Bell pole climber. Their two sons, John Jr. and Kenneth, and daughter, Mickey, made up a great family of which I am proud to have become a part. Now, Mother Black was a fine friend but I must admit that at times she could be quite a challenge. She had strong opinions and didn't abandon them easily. I'm proud to say that I could usually joke her out of the most off of the wall opinions and in all of those years we never had a serious confrontation.

After Dad Black's death in 1978 she remained in their home in Columbia, S.C. We visited often. John and Nick (Kenneth) were closer and provided strong support as the years went by. Toward the end of her life John arranged a very capable companion for her which permitted her to stay in her home until the end of her life in 1998 at the age of 99. I rejoice in her life especially because she brought me Mickey and because she was such a wonderful Grandmother for our daughters.

Ken Black (Nick) (Mickey's brother between John, Jr and Mickey) - As I mentioned earlier, Nick in World War II was a member of Patton's Third Army during and following the break out in Normandy until German surrender. He had a tough and dangerous job. An army on the move is heavily dependent upon the effectiveness of its supply lines. The enemy knows this and one of its prime objectives is to sever that line any way they can- bombing, strafing, counter attacks, sabotage- you name it. Nick was a truck driver in Patton's supply line. He experienced all of those activities and still came home alive. Yes, there were emotional scars which may or may not have contributed to the fact that at age 35 he was diagnosed with multiple sclerosis (MS). In spite of all that family and doctors could do he gradually declined in health and died in 1996, leaving behind his wife, Robbie, and 4 children.

John Black , JR ( Mickey's oldest brother) – As I write this I'm pleased to tell you that John and Dot are still with us living in Reidsville, NC: We just recently attended the wedding of a beautiful great granddaughter of theirs , Diana, in Panama City (near Destin). During World War II John, Jr worked in a ship building company and after that had a fine career with Rheem Manufacturing Co. He is almost a true copy of his father- smart, hardworking, great sense of humor and just fun to be with. We are good friends.

2005 – Quint – As I have written earlier, my youngest brother, Quint, was a very successful doctor in Florence, AL and Snowmass, CO. His life had been an interesting one - It would make a fine movie. With Ann Cook, his first wife, he was the father of three wonderful children - Anne Katherine, Quintus Cook and Dorothy. They and their children play a major role in helping to keep our reunions going. And young Quint, Jr, my Godson, is the one who gave Swanky II (The Canoe) to me. Brother Quint and his wife, Irina, decided to retire and move to Ashville, NC. It would be closer to his family and to friends from his Duke University days as well as his brothers.

They were happily settled when Quint realized that he was in early stage Parkinson's disease. He lingered for a couple of years before dying in 2005. We all miss him.

2008 – Charles Poole – By now you have read a little about Charles - He was our first son-in-law (Trish's husband). Without my knowledge he started to work in one of my divisions at Genesco and went on to have a fine career in the footwear industry. He fathered two wonderful grandchildren. He was my work partner on the farm. He and I took a great trip into the Boundary Waters together. He was truly like a son to me. When he was diagnosed with cancer we were together with Trish and Charles often. On his final day Trish, Sam, Krista, Mickey and his sister Diane and I stood by his bed as he drew his last breath. His parents arrived shortly after. We all loved him dearly and miss him more than I can describe.

## The Discussion Group

During my first couple of years at General Shoe Corporation I was invited to participate in a speakers training program called "The Speechmasters". As a part of the program we had to create and present a speech to the class which would then evaluate your effort and provide constructive comments or sometimes brutal criticisms. It was very helpful and we made much progress.

When my class ended, those of us in the class decided that we wanted to continue this fine training on our own so we began meeting regularly as "The Toast Masters". Before long our wives began to complain about this "boys night out" so we decided to invite them to join what we dubbed the "Discussion Group". We expanded the group by inviting non - Genesco friends to join. Before long we had a terrific, very diverse group of 15 couples: Several Genesco Execs, Doctors, Lawyers, Business Owners, Insurance Execs, Interior Designer, etc. and we adopted a new format. Two couples (rotated each time) would be responsible for the program. It could be whatever they wished but had to provide opportunities for the two couples and their audience to participate and get practice in communicating. Wow! What a flood of fantastic programs this created ranging from the deadly serious to the hilarious! It was one of the finest ways to get to know and cherish a wonderful group of friends for over fifty years. And we had fun! Like the murder which occurred and had to be investigated and solved; the in depth analysis of the first men in space activity; performance of a New York musical, etc. etc.

As we got older and older we had more and more guest speakers. This really broadened the horizon on subjects. For example - the clairvoyant (presented by one of our doctors) who could see into the past and future. I was selected for a "Life Reading". After quite an accurate summary of some of my background (which Dr. Bill Wadlington could have provided her - he says he didn't!☺) she started to go back, back, back into my previous lives. Yep, you read it right!

First, I was a field hand on an estate in Central Asia, and then I was a hermit living in a cave in the Middle East. Well, this didn't impress me. But then she said "I see you in a beautiful city with many remarkable buildings. Everyone is dressed in white robe like garments. You are going up the steps of one these beautiful buildings and entering the door. It's the Roman Senate Building!"

Well, this really got my attention! A couple of years before Mickey and I had taken our girls on the "Grand Tour of Europe". When we got to Rome our guide had let us roam around by ourselves. And daughter Trish and I saw a beautiful building and decided to get a closer look. We walked up the steps and opened this wide door. I stepped inside and stopped cold! I had been there before! And I said, "Trish! I have been here before. This is the Roman Senate! Senator_____ (And I gave a name) sat there. I sat over there!" And Trish said "Daddy, be still. You are scaring the _____ out of me! "But it was very real to me!

Was the Clairvoyant right? Well, I guess I won't know until the next time around! ☺

The "Discussion Group" has over many years been a terrific activity for us - crossroad? You call it!

# Chapter 15

## Crossroad Jewels in Retirement

- Swanky II

- Consulting

- The Life and Times of Quintus Quincy Quigley

- The Sponsors Scholarship Program

- Tennessee Angles Farm on the Market

- Mickey

## Swanky II

You may remember that in the early pages of "Crossroads" I told you about my Dad proposing to Mom in his canoe. Well, that canoe has been a part of our family life since 1924. After Dad's death in 1965 Brother Quint took the canoe to his home on the Tennessee River outside Florence, Alabama where it served his family for many years. Shortly after I retired from F.I.A., Quint, Jr called to talk with me about the canoe which after 63 years was in terrible shape and asked if I and would I like to have it. So I went to Florence and brought it to Nashville. Holy Smokes! When Quint said "terrible shape" that was a considerable understatement. It was ready for a burial.

So, what to do!? After a very close inspection I decided to consider repairing it. Trish and Charles were now living in New Hampshire only a short distance from Old Town Canoe Co. in Maine where the canoe was built in 1923. On our next visit Mickey and I drove over for a visit to Old Town. What an eye opener! In addition to their modern canoes they still made the old wooden canoes like ours. And when, at their request, I gave them the canoe's serial number they looked in their files and pulled out the very factory "ticket" that accompanied our canoe through the factory in 1923! Then I got a detailed tour through the factory, guided by John Hardesty, their expert on wooden canoes. For the next year he was my mentor by phone and helped me over many challenges.

And for the next year every spare hour from the farm was spent on repairing – oops - rebuilding the canoe. Mom insisted on paying for the materials ordered from Old Town and I did the work. Since my Dad's nickname was "Swanky" I named the canoe "Swanky II". After it was finished it looked like new! I was one proud guy! We took it to Langstaff Landing where it now lives. When we are there it rests on the dock on the 55 acre lake behind the cottage. It has helped catch many fish. Mom visited and had a special commemoration ride in "Her" canoe. What great memories!

As a crossroad I will attest that Swanky II has introduced many non-canoers to the fine and joyous art of canoeing- (including me!)

## Consulting

Shortly after we got resettled in Nashville I had a call from Tom Gleason, CEO of Wolverine World Wide Inc. (Hush Puppies+) a longtime friend and a Board member of F.I.A. The gist of the call was that he had some puzzling management issues and wondered if I would be willing to spend a few days with him in Grand Rapids to give him my thoughts and suggestions. I went. We met several of his key execs. I spent a couple of days meeting individually with each of them. We identified several issues and got them resolved.

He then decided that regular visits would be helpful and we agreed on 3 days a month (the maximum permitted by my boss – Mickey). And for fifteen years I visited Wolverine World Wide Inc. and counseled with their senior management team. This continued after Tom retired and Geof Bloom became CEO. After 15 years it was time for me to really retire (I was 72) and most of the team I started with were no longer active. And, frankly, I was no longer as industry-wise as I had been 15 years before. We parted with mutual respect.

Along the way I also responded to a few other consulting assignments but Wolverine World Wide Inc. was my favorite. I had really enjoyed this relationship and I do believe that our relationship was productive. And it was good for me also.

## The Life and Times of Quintus Quincy Quigley

My great grandfather Quintus Quincy Quigley (1872-1910) was a lawyer and state senator of note in Kentucky. Beginning in 1858 and continuing until 1908 he maintained a journal in which he recorded regularly his activities and his observations of events around him. Ultimately this journal was contained in three hand written volumes which were preserved by my Aunt Faith (Dad's oldest sister). After her death in 1955 Mom arranged for the Nashville Public Library to care for the journals. In the early 1960's Dad and I began to struggle with deciphering Quintus Quincy Quigley's very difficult handwriting. Dad helped me a lot but, unfortunately his life ended before we made much progress. And also my business and family life left me with no time to work on the journals. Several years after I retired in 1986 and we returned to Nashville I asked Mom to retrieve the journals and let me start on them again. And for 14 years Mickey and I worked as a team to "translate" these fascinating journals. In 1999 we published for our extended family an impressive 305 page book The Life and Times of Quintus Quincy Quigley. We also provided copies to a number of libraries, museums, schools, etc. The reactions were so positive that we then, in partnership with the Community Foundation of Western Kentucky, did a second commercial version. Proceeds from the sales were used to provide scholarships to the West Kentucky Community and Technical College located near Quintus Quincy Quigley's home (The Angles) for students from McCracken, Graves and Hickman Counties (Paducah, Mayfield and Clinton, KY) .The three original journals now rest in the Filson Club, Kentucky's Premier History Museum, in Louisville, Kentucky.

I view this project as a prime family historical crossroad. Our family now has clear knowledge of one of its most interesting and successful ancestors and Kentucky history has new insight into past events.

## The Sponsor Scholarship Program

By 1995 I had become a true farmer. My farm buddies had taught me how to do it all. Well I must admit they still laughed a lot at some of our "different" ways. But I now was doing my share of what needed to be done.

Early June was the prime haying season so we always returned from Langstaff Landing in time for the start of "haying". And in early June of 1995 I was at the farm early and ready to start cutting hay. If you have ever cut hay you know that it is one boring job! You go round and round and round the field. All you have to do is guide the tractor and not go to sleep. After about 6 hours of this I was really bored. So the idea came to me that I should begin to think about some serious national problem and work on how to solve it.

After a couple of hours on this project I had a key problem defined. "Too many of our young people fail to obtain an education adequate to permit them to compete effectively in the market place." So back to the hay. "Whoa!" the voice in my head said "What are you going to do about it?!" And I thought back "I'm just thinking, not doing."

But the "What are you going to do about it?" kept after me. Later in the summer we were on that terrific tour to Alaska and I was sitting by myself on the deck of the "Spirit of Alaska" watching that great scenery. All of a sudden it came again "What are you going to do about it?!" So I went down to our cabin and told Mickey about the whole thing. She was Okay about me working on something when we got home if that's what I wanted to do. And what I had decided to do was start a college scholarship program focused on our financially disadvantaged students.

Now what? This was a complex problem. A solution would require a lot of things - What is our student criteria? How do we raise the money? Where do we find the candidates? How do we evaluate and select them? Etc.

First off I knew I couldn't possibly undertake this by myself so I made a list of friends who might be motivated to join in the effort. It took a while but I wound up with nine couples willing to make a major financial commitment. While having lunch with Walter and Margaret Ann Robinson I mentioned that it looked like the money would come OK but the question would now be how to find the students. Margaret Ann then said "My nephew, Bill Weaver, knows how. Go see him."

The next day I went to see Bill. That was a true crossroad! Here was a man who in the middle of a successful business career came down with multiple sclerosis at the age of 35. He was now severely handicapped. In spite of that, he founded and ran a terrific program – Time to Rise- which provided summertime programs for disadvantaged 5th and 6th graders. We talked and talked. He understood the challenges of getting a new charity (501c3) online and suggested that we set it up as another program of Time to Rise. It would be easy to get the 501(c)3 approval as a new Time to Rise Program. Betty Ridgeway could be our Administrative Assistant as well as serving Time to Rise. This may have been the greatest crossroad of all! Betty knows everything and helped us solve many problems.

We started The Sponsors as a program of Time to Rise and with nine committed contributors. A fortunate visit that I made to the Community Foundation of Middle Tennessee allowed me to meet the Metro Director of Guidance Counselors Pat Cole which led to a great entre to Metro Schools, the primary source of the students we were looking for. We were off and running!

Originally, The Sponsors invited nominations from high schools and youth organizations of only Davidson County Tennessee, but later good friend Laura Turner Dugas, a Florida neighbor, invited us to include her home county, Allen County, KY. which she would finance from her mother's foundation. Thirty eight of our over three hundred and thirty students have come from Allen County (Scottsville) KY. We also now include Wilson and Williamson Counties of Middle Tennessee.

And we operated as a part of Time to Rise until Bill's health made it necessary for us to obtain our own 501(c) 3 and move our administrative work out of the Weaver home. I will never forget Bill Weaver- one of the finest men I have ever known.

We employed a part time secretary - Nancy Duvier- to handle the work that Betty had been doing. Here again we were blessed. Nancy has been a true joy for The Sponsors. She is passionate about our students and she does her job very well. Her extensive teaching experience makes her a truly valuable member of our team.

I am so proud of The Sponsors and the many volunteers (over 250) who have made this program successful. Over 350 students have been assisted, 64% graduation rate, less than 5 % overhead, all students from very difficult backgrounds (Pell Grant Eligible). We also provide friendship mentors for students who want one. The mentors are not to teach a subject but just to give the student a friend to help them in the transition to college.

Our Board (all volunteers) consists of men and women from very successful backgrounds- senior business executives, bankers, lawyers, teachers, librarian, and accountant. About 18 months ago shortly after I reached 85, I wrote a letter to the Board which recognized the fact that I was getting old. Or as some would say- I was already old! Since I was spending some 30 hours/week on the program the reality was that we should consider a strategy for the future.

One- We could phase the program down and out.

Two – We could transition to new leadership and keep going

Should they vote for # 2 I would appoint a "Future Vision" Committee to develop the transmission plan. They unanimously voted for # 2.

The "New Vision Committee" was appointed, came up with a plan and the new Board under the leadership of Garry Sharp, a retired AT&T executive, is doing great. I have great confidence in the future of The Sponsors. I hope the Lord is happy with what I "tried to do about it!"

Mickey and I will continue to serve on the scholarship committee and provide financial support. I am honored that the board has asked me to remain as Chairman Emeritus.

## Congressional Recognition

In mid-September 2012 as I sorted through the day's mail I found an invitation to a reception honoring George Langstaff for his work in initiating and managing The Sponsors Scholarship Program. The United States House of Representative on September 10, 2012, at the initiative of Representative Jim Cooper, had entered a citation in the "Congressional Record" to this effect. The Sponsors Board of Directors had organized the reception at which Rep. Jim Cooper would make the presentation of a plaque to me. What a surprise! Frankly, I was bowled over!

The reception at the beautiful Danner Home was truly impressive with a large number of Sponsor participants, contributors, students, graduates; members of our family, etc. Rep. Jim Cooper's remarks revealed a genuine understanding of our program and of what Mickey and I with over 250 volunteers have worked so hard to accomplish. He also recognized the intention of our many volunteers and contributors to carry the program forward aggressively.

It was one special afternoon which I'm sure was secretly initiated by The Sponsors Board even though they haven't admitted it. ☺

### Tennessee Angles Farm on the Market

After many years of farming, weekending, fly fishing, hunting, gardening etc. it was apparent that my days as a farmer were about to end. We began to consider our sale strategy. The farm was divided into 2 segments by a creek. The larger segment had a 1 ½ acre lake, a nice pond, the barn and sheds and the cottage and another shed. It had 120 acres. The smaller track had 15 acres, was on the road and could be divided into three road front lots of 5 acres each. So we offered a 120 acre farm and three lots. We were in Florida when I got a call from Johnny Green whose family had worked on the farm since we bought it. He said that he was at the farm burning the pile of brush we had piled up and a couple had come through the gate and asked if they could take a look at the farm. He just wanted me to know that we had a visitor. So I asked if he had gotten their phone number and he said "Well, he's standing right here." And that's how I "met" Wayne Anderson.

As soon as we got home we met Wayne, his wife, Kelley and their very cute twins. He made an offer on the large tract, we countered and he accepted. I then made a proposal for the entire 15 acre tract so that it could remain a better cattle farm and he accepted that offer. Tennessee Angles Farm was sold. And it was sold to a couple that we like very much. They love the farm like we did. They now have a third child and "The Gang" is on the farm regularly. One of Wayne's first actions after he changed the gate locks at the farm was to bring me a set of the new keys and urge us to come out anytime.

I can hardly begin to express how much the farm meant to us over the 35 years we owned it. There were so many good things- The great friends we made in the neighborhood, the joy of weekends, the garden , fishing, hunting, benefit of hard physical work, fun of running farm machinery and, of course, the capital gain from the sale.

## Mickey

I first saw Mickey Black in the Fall of 1944, met her in February 1945 and we were married on December 27, 1946. We have now celebrated our 66th Anniversary. Over those many years we have gone through incredible adventures which often tested our relationship but never broke it. I have deep respect and love for her! If you could watch her walk into a lunch room filled with assisted living folks who seem to have no energy or interest and then see what happens when she sits at the piano (without music) and starts to play the songs from "the good old days" you would be impressed. Within a few minutes there is a total change in the audience – foot tapping, singing and even dancing. Facial expressions go from gloomy to joyful and excited. And Mickey has done this weekly for <u>many</u> years in Nashville, Gallatin, and Destin, Florida.

She has done a wonderful job of birthing and raising our three daughters and being a loyal and devoted wife to a husband who has been almost constantly under enormous challenges. During all these years she has been a loyal community volunteer - St. Luke's Thrift Shop, Vanderbilt Hospital Gifts shop,, Parent- Teachers Organizations, Girl Scout Leader, Etc.

In our business moves to Massachusetts, Kentucky and Pennsylvania, she accepted the challenges and helped make them work. In the ups and downs of my business career I have never had to doubt her support. When we undertook complex challenges she was right there with me to be my strong partner whether it was tennis, producing the Quintus Quincy Quigley book, planning our " World Travel" plan, building two houses, running the farm, raising the daughters, and on and on.

Have we had differences? Yep! But we work through them and every day I thank the Lord for my wife and best friend. Together we have created a family including 6 grandchildren and 7 (so far) great grands of whom we are very proud.

# Chapter 16

"For unto whomsoever much is given of him shall be much required"

St. Luke 12:48

- A Wrap Up

- "My Grandfather"- Todd Frederick

- Adieu

## A Wrap Up

As I sit here at my desk reviewing what has been written I look up at a large survey map of Tennessee Angles Farm over which I have attached dozens of photographs of family, friends, events, places, pets, etc. They range from Great Grandfather's pictures and journals to our latest (of 7) great grandchildren – Caroline; Events cover almost everything I have written about. Also in frames around the walls are framed testimonials in my honor for accomplishments made.

I will rest my case for a wonderful life on a 5th grade essay by my grandson Todd Frederick (10) at Eura Brown Elementary School in Gadsden, Alabama. This is the same grandson who practices law in Gadsden, Alabama. He and wife, Dr. Lindsay, are Caroline's parents. I copied the following word for word from his original paper which I have framed.

This is also the same grandson who after helping me rake and bale hay on the farm  wrote me a " Thank you letter" which wound up saying " ... and it helped me decide that when I am grown I don't want to be a farmer." ☺

## My Grandfather

"My Grandfather is special to me. He'll play games with me if I'm bored. He tells stories that are interesting, funny and good. My Grandfather gives me things and makes me things. He made me a hiking stick a couple of years ago that I still use.

My Grandfather is funny and smart. He taught me to play chess. When he plays me in a game he never goes easy on me. He'll take me to fun museums and exhibits. Also he'll show me the major tourist attractions of a town. One time he showed me around the college he went to in South Carolina and he showed me the place he first kissed my Grandmother.

My Grandfather's stories are very good. He can tell me stories my Mother doesn't remember. One time he told me about when he and my Mother went ice fishing. He said my Mother got so cold she froze stiff. Also, he told me about one time when a flood came to Padukah (sic), Kentucky his birthplace. He said that someone stole their canoe so they could not get around. So my Great Grandfather went out, found the canoe and brought it back.

My Grandfather loves me and respects me. He is kind, gentle and stern. But most of all he is great, wonderful and a super guy!" -Todd Frederick, 10, 5th Grade

122

### Adieu

In all of the foregoing I have attempted to give the readers insight into a life lived with joys, sorrows, challenges, successes, failures, poverty and plenty , failing in love but also world  class success in love, a close knit and devoted family, many interests to keep one busy and a lifelong devotion to Christianity. St. Luke's message which leads this chapter is the challenge which we all face and the challenge which I sometimes have met and sometimes have failed to meet. I can only hope and pray that the final score favors "Met". I also hope the Lord will read Todd's letter. ☺

George Quigley Langstaff, Jr.

# Photographs

Mom, Dad and Baby George, Jr. – 1925

"Hey! We've Just Been Married."
Grandfather Langstaff's handout to train boarders.
(See addendums)

Mom and Dad at Sharondale Court – 1950's

Mom and Dad at the cabin – 1940's

Mom, Quint, Johnnie Pierson – 1970's

Katherine and George Langstaff in their prime

Mom in her later years

Mable and John Black, Mickey's Mom and Dad

# SECTION 2 – PADUCAH HOME AND THE CABIN

*244 N. 38th St – My "Growing Up Home"*

*The Cabin – Witt and Quint*

*The Cabin – Mom and sister Mermie*

*The Cabin – George, Quint, Witt and Jack*

*The Cabin – Quint and Lazy George*

*Showing Off – Don Mulligan, George, Frank Nagel, Tommy, Sue Langstaff, Lou Rutter*

*Our Canoe with Mom, the Boys and Jack*

*Local Indians – George, Witt and Quint*

*The Mill – Flood of 1937*

*Dad Elder (The Old Fisherman),
Dad, His Sons & Tommy*

*Cousin Tommy Langstaff and George*

*Avondale Guards – George, Hunter Martin, Tommy,
Quint, Stanley Tick, Frank Nagel*

*Three George Langstaffs*

*George and Bob Tindall –
NROTC, Univ. of South Carolina*

*Mickey Black, George, Sara Cline
1945*

*University of the South – Chapel
(Sewanee)*

*The Motor Vessel Celeste – Mississippi River – 1946*

*George, Hi Haynie – Empire State Bldg, NY – 1947*

*Green's View, Sewanee – Mickey, George, Lynne – 2010*

*QUEEN BLACK Accedes*

# ........ Rain!

# The 1946 MAY DAY

Springtime, the custom of having a Queen of the May, a bevy of lovely co-eds seeking excitement, and politics pervading the air, all conspired for a beauty pageant and election, and another Queen of the May.

After the KSK sponsored beauty pageant wily politicians left behind-the-scenes "wire" pulling to the girl politicians.

Tallying of the ballots showed that Mickey Black had taken the race. Phyllis Karesh won over Betty Hendley for the place of maid-of-honor.

Members of the court were Betty Ann Moody, Trudie Leonard, Libby Duncan, Bettie Moore, Laura Speed, Bert Hemingway, Sally Rickman, Jinx Giles, Mary Shoun, Nell Mayer, Dolores Allen, Betty Lou Hood, Nancy Nash, Dolores Schuler, Betty Bunch, Vivian Anderson, Cathy Geraty, Betty Childs, Leslie Bennett, and Ruth Burns.

Also Eleanor Bonds, Irene Hugenin, Frances Lee, Jo Morton, Miriam Summersett, Pinky Bartlett, Carolyn Bean, Sara Jean Baldwin, Lynn Efron, Beverly George, Mary Knowles, Adelaide Sox, Sara Cline, Harriet Cohen, Jeanne Early, Penny Jennings, Gretchen Gayden and Ann Ford.

Pages were Jean Badger and Lucy Jane Owings.

*May Queen – University of South Carolina – 1946*

Mickey the Bride

George and Mickey – Happy Bride & Groom 1946

*The Bridal Party – Washington Street Methodist Church*
*1st Row – Dad, Mom, George, Mickey, Mom & Dad Black*
*2nd Row – Gloria Widener, Sue Langstaff, Jeanne Early, Witt, Beverly Hutto,*
*Mary Louis Howard, "Dinky" Bradford*
*3rd Row – Ken Black, Howard House, John Black, Don Fitzgerald, Quint*

Our early family and Mom at Loveless Motel

Our girls with the Witts at Brookfield Drive

The Quints & the Georges with moms Anne & Mickey

Mickey and her girls

Mickey and George without hair

The Pooles – Charles, Trish, Sam and Krista

My Girl

The Fredericks – Todd, Caroline, Lindsay, Steve,
Lynne, Scott and Alana

The Stockmans – Greg, Chris Worley, Taylor Worley,
George, Jennifer and Matthew Worley, Kathy

The Langstaff Brothers, Witt, Quint, George

The Langstaff Brothers and Wives Mickey, Helen,
Irina at Langstaff Landing

The Witt Langstaffs – Witt Jr., Jamie, George,
Sara, Lindy, Helen, Witt

*Tommy Langstaff – Portrait by Witt*

*Quint, Anne and Family*
*Quint, Quint Jr., Dorothy, Anne, Katherine, Anne*

*George and Mickey – Dressed Up*

*George and Mickey – Dressed Down*

John Black, Jr. and Family
Diana, Tom, Janet, Ian, Dorothy, Kenny,
Zan, Sophie, John Jr., Mickey

Kenneth (Nick) Black

John Blacks

Kenny Black and Family
Kenny, Michele, Zan, Sophie, Trevor

*Our 50th Anniversary – Cancun, Mexico 1997*
*Scott, Trish, Charles, Sam, Steve, Lynne, Mickey, George, Kathy, George, Todd, Krista, Jennifer, Greg*

*Our six grandchildren at the anniversary*
*Todd, Sam, Scott, Greg, Jennifer, Krista*

*Langstaff-Pierson Reunion (with Mom)*

*Langstaff-Pierson Reunion (without Mom)*

Langstaff-Irion Reunion (Colorado)

Langstaff-Irion Reunion (Paducah)

The Discussion Group

Charm Step

The Bridge Club

14

*George at work with U.S. Senators and Representatives*
*1982-1986*

*6001 Andover*

*Langstaff Landing, Santa Rosa Beach, FL*

*Langstaff Landing, Coffeen Lake (North View)*

*Four Mile Village Beach – East Across the Topsail Hill State Preserve*

*Four Mile Village Beach (Gulf of Mexico)*

*Swanky II*

*Swanky II on Coffeen Lake (89 Years Old)*

*Tennessee Angles Farm, Williamson County, TN*

*Tennessee Angles Farm, The Entry*

*Tennessee Angles Farm, Cottage and Barn*

*Tennessee Angles Farm*
*Welcoming the Wayne Andersons, the new owners –*
*Wayne, Kelly and the twins.*
*Welcoming Team: Todd Frederick, Mickey, Trish,*
*Steve and Lynne Frederick*

*The Pooles – Sam, Tracy, Jay and Reese*
*Ready to Ride*

*Jay – A Farmer to Be*

17

*The Sam Pooles – Jay, Sam, Tracy, Reese*

*Great Grand #7 – Caroline Frederick*

*The Worley Family – Jennifer, Chris, Taylor, Matthew
at Langstaff Landing*

*Greg with Carey Foster (now Mrs. Greg Haag)*

*Scott with Alana Crowe
(soon to be Mrs. Scott Frederick)*

*The Carpenedos*
*Mike, Krista, Emmy and Kaia*

*The Stockmans, Worleys and Haags*
*Greg, Carey, Jennifer, Chris,*
*Taylor, George, Kathy and Matthew*

## SECTION 11 – MICKEY PLAYS

*The Canadian Quetico – First Trip 1951*

*Grand Canyon with our Daughters – 1962*

*Venice, Italy – 1969*

*Switzerland – 1969*

*Wimbledon – 1986*

*Switzerland – Our Means of Travel*

*Lunch Break in Russia – 1989 (with Witt & Helen)*

*Gougane Barra – Ireland 1996*

*Berlin Wall – Sept. 1989 (just before it came down)*

*Langstaff Intake, Healaugh, England 1997*
*The home of my ancestors before immigration*

*St. Ives, England 1997*

*Healaugh on the Swale – View from Langstaff Intake*

*Quetico with Greg*

21

Quetico – Old George

Shanghai Airport – 1998 – Zhou Qian Qian and Family

"Our Delta Queen"
with Haynes (St. Louis to Minneapolis)
with Castners (Memphis to New Orleans)

Mont San Michel, France 2001 (with Hancocks)

Yellowstone National Park (with Hancocks)

Bill Weaver and George Langstaff
Together we started The Sponsors Scholarship Program

The Sponsors Board of Directors –
Garry Sharp, Wills Oglesby, Darnell Clay, Charles
Bryan, George Langstaff, Larry Shelton, Kay Evans,
Nancy Duvier, Sec., Harriet Dunn, Mindy Brown

Sponsor Friends – Mickey, Laura Dugas,
George, Wayne Dugas

Garry Sharp Chairs the Scholarship Committee Meeting

Scholarship Committee at Work

An interview team with nominating guidance counselors at Allen County, KY High School
Dave Thomas, George Langstaff, Jane Yokley, Melissa
Williams, Paige Tabor, Dr. Ronnie Pridemore (one of
our students from several years back)

# Congressional Record

PROCEEDINGS AND DEBATES OF THE 112th CONGRESS, SECOND SESSION

WASHINGTON, MONDAY, SEPTEMBER 10, 2012

## House of Representatives

### HONORING GEORGE LANGSTAFF

**HON. JIM COOPER**
OF TENNESSEE
IN THE HOUSE OF REPRESENTATIVES
*Monday, September 10, 2012*

Mr. COOPER. Mr. Speaker, I rise today to pay tribute to George Langstaff, a man whose dedication to mentoring economically disadvantaged students in Middle Tennessee has resulted in more than 340 students obtaining a post-high school education.

After a very successful career in the footwear industry, Mr. Langstaff recognized the need to help at-risk young adults obtain a college education. In 1995, he partnered with a Nashville nonprofit to found The Sponsors Scholarship Program. To date, the program that Mr. Langstaff established has raised more than $2.2 million dedicated to scholarships for financially disadvantaged young people.

For more than 15 years, The Sponsors Scholarship Program and its hundreds of volunteers have provided college counseling, mentoring and college scholarships to capable high school students in Middle Tennessee.

Today, I join the citizens of my district in honoring George Langstaff for his tireless commitment to ensuring that financially challenged young people from Middle Tennessee have the opportunity to obtain a complete education.

We need more citizens like George Langstaff. His Volunteer Spirit makes all Tennesseans proud, and a generation of young people successful.

*The U.S. House of Representatives recognizes George Langstaff and The Sponsors Scholarship Program*

*Congressman Jim Cooper presents the award*

24

GROWING UP HOME

THE CABIN

6001 ANDOVER DR.

LANGSTAFF LANDING

TENNESSEE ANGLES

# Addendums

# Hey!
## We've Just Been Married

And want to tell you now that we are **GOOD SPORTS** so come on and show us just how a loving pair of newlyweds should be handled.

We are going to ride this train with you folks in the Drawing Room of the Chicago Pullman - and don't want to be left alone. This is an invitation to come and get acquainted so don't be backward - we are not in the least afflicted that way and **CRAVE COMPANY**.

Anyway we make a darn good looking couple so come and take a look at least.

Mr. and Mrs. George Quigley Langstaff

# OLD GEORGE'S IDEAS ABOUT CAREER SELECTION

Careful, intelligent career selection will make a major, positive difference in your life. Consideration of the following questions/points may help a young graduate crystallize a career selection plan of action.

1.   What do you really like to do?

2.   What are you really good at doing?

3.   What marketable skills do you have?

4.   What career paths does all of this suggest?

5.   What organizations could offer attractive job opportunities in your field of interest?
     
     or
     
     What additional education/training do you need in order to qualify for such opportunities?

6.   If you're ready for employment how do you craft your resume to make you an attractive commodity?

7.   What organizations are your top employment (or training) targets?

8.   Do you have contacts with the "targets?"

9.   How do you utilize these contacts?

10.  Establish a comprehensive plan of action and a timetable for measuring progress.

11.  Be diligent - but patient - in working your plan.


Old George

### OLD GEORGE'S POINTS FOR A NEW EXECUTIVE TO CONSIDER

1. Don't signal that you expect to be the CEO tomorrow. Signal that you are a team player who wants to learn the business and will work hard and intelligently to help it prosper.

2. Do become a student of the business you have joined. What's it all about? How does it function? What are its strengths and weaknesses? Etc.

3. Take every assignment with gusto and do it better than it's ever been done before.

4. Listen carefully to the assignment and make sure you understand - don't hesitate to ask questions. Don't assume you know it all.

5. Be honest and reliable.

6. Be humble but confident.

7. Keep your sense of humor.

8. Leave bragging behind - let your results speak for you.

9. Work your tail off.

10. Never lose your temper.

11. Develop reasonable patience.

12. Study the executive to whom you report:
    - If he/she is top flight you will learn a lot
    - If he/she is lousy learn from the weaknesses

13. When given the opportunity, express well-reasoned opinions - do it with thoughtful confidence - not with bravado.

14. When your ideas are challenged, listen with care and open mindedness. If you're wrong, acknowledge it and adopt a corrected position with grace.

15. Treat all associates with respect.

16. Accept accountability for your failures and embrace constructive criticism.

17. Be a team builder. There are limits to what one individual can accomplish alone. There are no limits to what an individual working effectively through and with others can accomplish.

18. Set aside regular time for rest and relaxation
    - With family
    - With friends
    - Quiet time alone

    (No person can work all the time without time to "recharge the batteries.")

    Old George

# OLD GEORGE'S
# FINANCIAL PLAN FOR LIFE

## LIFETIME STRATEGY

1. Live below your financial means
2. Save at least 10% of pre-tax income
3. Invest it wisely in a broad base of real estate, annuities, mutual funds, gold and carefully selected stocks
4. Maintain a substantial liquid reserve (minimum one year of living expense)
5. Contribute at least 10% of income to church and charities annually

## RETIREMENT OBJECTIVE

By age 60 be ready to retire with:

A. Locked in annual income from annuities, retirement income, dividends, etc. equal to the actual portion of our income which we have been consuming for the last five years
B. Investments in securities, real estate, mutual funds, savings, etc. of sufficient worth to offset future foreseeable inflation
C. Emergency fund of at least $75,000 cash (FDIC protected)

## THE RICHEST MAN IN BABYLON

Read and absorb the wealth management secrets of the ancients as described in the inspiring book "The Richest Man in Babylon" - George S. Clason, 1926.

My dad started telling me about this book when I was a teenager. I strongly recommend it.

# MORE THAN YOU EVER WANTED TO KNOW ABOUT

## GEORGE Q. LANGSTAFF, JR.

## EMPLOYMENT HISTORY

**1976 - 2010**  **Farmer**
Owned and operated cattle farm in Williamson County, TN.  (Black Angus)  Learned to do it all - Fencing, Bushogging, Cutting, Raking and Baling Hay; Doctoring Cattle, etc., etc.  Loved it!!

**2/1/86 - 2001**  **Management Consultant to the Footwear Industry**

**11/1/81 - 2/1/86**  **President & CEO - Footwear Industries of America**
Oversaw the footwear association that resulted from the merger of American Shoe Center with American Footwear Industries Association.

**11/1/81 - 2/1/86**  **Board of Directors - SATRA, Inc. - Northallerton, England**

**2/1/81 - 11/1/81**  **President - American Shoe Center**
Directed a footwear technology association created to assist the American footwear manufacturers and suppliers.

**1977 - 1980**  **Executive Vice President, General Manager - Genesco Footwear**
Headed all Genesco Footwear activities.

**1974 - 1977**  **Vice President, Group President - Genesco Footwear**
Headed all Genesco Footwear activities except International.

**1972 - 1974**  **Vice President, Group President - Genesco Footwear Marketing & Manufacturing**
Headed Domestic Footwear Wholesale and Manufacturing operations (except Retail and Supply)

**1969 - 1972**  **Vice President, Director - Genesco Footwear Marketing**
Headed Footwear Wholesale Product, Sales and Physical Distribution.

**1963 - 1969**  **Assistant to Director of Genesco Footwear Marketing and Manufacturing**
Gradually assumed marketing responsibility during this period.

**1959 - 1963**  **President - Charm Step Shoe Co.**
Conducted market study and established new Genesco company to manufacture and market popular priced women's shoes.  Rapid growth and high profitability.

**1948 - 1959**  **Positions of Increasing Responsibility - Genesco Footwear Manufacturing**

## ACADEMIC & MILITARY

### PRE COLLEGE

Brazelton Junior High - Paducah, KY
- **Senior Class President**

Tilghman High School - Paducah, KY
Class of 1943
- **Junior Class President**
- **Student Body President Senior Year**
- **East-West Shrine Bowl (Football), 1942**
- **All-Southern Football, 1942**
- **Kentucky Debate - State Runners Up and Regional Champs, 1943**

## ACADEMIC & MILITARY *continued*

### COLLEGES

| | |
|---|---|
| 1943 - 1944 | Emory University - Navy V-12 |
| 1944 - 1945 | University of South Carolina - Navy R.O.T.C. |
| 1945 - 1946 | U.S. Naval Academy - Midshipman |
| 1946 - 1948 | University of the South at Sewanee - Bachelor of Arts - Optime Merens |

### COLLEGE ACTIVITIES

- University of South Carolina Varsity Football
- University of the South
  - Fraternity President - Sigma Nu
  - ODK
  - Blue Key
  - Honor Council President
  - Economics Major

### POST COLLEGE

| | |
|---|---|
| 1959 | M.I.T. - Marketing Strategy and Tactics |
| 1962 | University of Michigan - Modern Management Principles |
| 1964 | AMA - Marketing |
| 1965 | University of Michigan - Consumer Behavior |
| 1968 | Dorothy Sarnoff - Speech Dynamics |
| 1978 | Harvard Business School - Advanced Management Program |

### MILITARY

| | |
|---|---|
| 1943 - 1946 | U.S. Navy |

## FOOTWEAR INDUSTRY ACTIVITIES

- American Footwear Industries Association - Director and Executive Committee, 1972
- National Shoe Fair - Chairman, 1971
- AFIA Marketing Committee - Chairman, 1970

## CIVIC AND RELIGIOUS ACTIVITY

- Boy Scout Troop Leader - Burton School, Nashville
- St. George's Episcopal Church - Vestry (5 Terms), Senior Warden (3 Terms)
- Episcopal Churchmen of Tennessee - President
- Nashville Mental Health Association - President and Director
- Junior Achievement - Director
- United Fund of Nashville - Director and Executive Committee
- University of the South - Trustee
- Citizens For The Preservation of "Topsail Hill" - Walton County, Florida
  - Organized and led efforts to preserve 1800 acre pristine coastal region. Resulted in the preservation of this spectacular tract plus 18,000 acres of additional non-coastal land in Walton County.

## CIVIC AND RELIGIOUS ACTIVITY *continued*

- THE SPONSORS Scholarship Program
  - Founded this college scholarship program in 1996 which supports 80+ needy students each year in their quest for a college education.  338 assisted to date.
- Co-Presenter and Publisher of "The Life and Times of Quintus Quincy Quigley" in 1999 - the amazing journal of a noted West Kentucky attorney recording his life and significant events of the 19th century.
- Four Mile Village (Walton County, Florida) - Board of Directors (3 Terms) and President (3 Terms)
- Republican Party
  - Middle Tennessee Co-Campaign Manager of Eisenhower and Nixon Presidential Campaign, 1952
  - Elected to Tennessee State Republican Executive Committee, 1952
- Belle Meade Country Club

## MY FAMILY

The most important thing I have done over the years is to court and marry a beautiful and talented lady and create a wonderful family with her.  Mickey Black was drum majorette of The University of South Carolina band and May Queen when I played football for South Carolina.  She is a very talented piano player who for many years has volunteered her talents at assisted living facilities.  We met on a blind date and have been together 65 years.

Our three wonderful daughters, Trish, Lynne and Kathy, with their fine husbands, have blessed us with 6 grandchildren and seven great grandchildren.  In our own early years Mickey and George were both blessed with world class parents who guided our development with intelligence, firmness, patience, faith and tons of love.

## BIRTH

Born:   July 28, 1925 at Riverside Hospital, Paducah, KY
Parents: George Quigley and Katherine Irion Langstaff

## HOBBIES

- Tennis
- Golf
- Farming
- Fishing
- Canoeing

*    *    *    *    *

**LIFE HAS BEEN GOOD!  THANK YOU, LORD!**